KOREAN *through* ENGLISH

THE LANGUAGE RESEARCH INSTITUTE OF
SEOUL NATIONAL UNIVERSITY

한국어 1

HOLLYM
Elizabeth, NJ · Seoul

Korean through English 1

Copyright © 1993
by Ministry of Culture and Sports

All rights reserved

Originally published in November 1992
by Ministry of Culture and Sports

Second Edition
Second printing, 1997
by Hollym International Corp.
18 Donald Place, Elizabeth, NJ 07208 U.S.A.
Phone: (908)353-1655 Fax: (908)353-0255

Published simultaneously in Korea
by Hollym Corporation; Publishers
13-13 Kwanchol-dong, Chongno-gu, Seoul 110-111
Phone: (02)735-7554 Fax: (02)730-5149

ISBN: 1-56591-015-x(Book 1)
        1-56591-023-0(Tapes 1)
        1-56591-042-7(Audio package 1)
        1-56591-018-4(Book Set)
        1-56591-045-1(Audio package Set)
Library of Congress Catalog Card Number: 93-79442
Book Title & Cover Design © Hollym

Printed in Korea

Preface

1. This textbook was written by Sang-Oak Lee, Hi-Won Yoon, Jae-Young Han, Mee-Sun Han, and Eun-Gyu Choi at the Language Research Institute of Seoul National University. It comprises three volumes, with 25 lessons in each volume.

2. This textbook has been created under the following general guidelines for content:

   a) The content must be easy (in particular, vol. 1 and 2).

   b) It must be entertaining, as well as educational (particularly vol.3).

   c) It must reflect the phonological and grammatical characteristics of Korean.

   d) It must introduce aspects of Korean culture in a natural and unaffected way.

   e) It must enable individuals to study alone, without the aid of a teacher or classroom environment.

3. In order to meet the above guidelines, we have compiled a list of basic vocabulary items to be included in textbook. In this compilation we have relied on existing word frequency surveys, but have included some words out of their order in such surveys if they relate directly to the topic of the lesson. For the grammatical items, we first made a list of the grammatical morphemes of Korean, and then selected the most commonly used ones for inclusion in the textbook. As for pronunciation, we have listed and organized the various phonetic and phonological rules of Korean, and included drills for them as they appear in the text.

4. Lessons 1 through 5 of Volume 1 are devoted to the introduction and practice of the Korean alphabet *Han-gŭl*. This alphabet, invented more than 500 years ago (in 1443 to be exact) by King Sejong, is based on

careful observation of the phonological characteristics of the Korean language, and is perhaps the most scientific alphabet ever created. Students unfamiliar with it will find it very logical and easy to learn. Practice in writing the characters is included for familiarization with the structure of *Han-gŭl* Students are urged to pay close attention to stroke order, and to make sure that lines are evenly spaced and each syllable fits neatly within a square box.

5. Each lesson is made up of Vocabulary, Pronunciation, Main Text, Grammar, and Exercise sections.

In the Vocabulary section, the new words of the lesson are presented along with a brief gloss in English. These glosses provide a general idea of the meaning of the words; for more in-depth definitions students are encouraged to consult at good dictionary or a native speaker of Korean.

The Pronunciation sections single out vocabulary items which are unusual or which have proven particularly difficult for English speakers. The characteristic sounds of Korean should be learned accurately at an early stage, to prevent the formation of bad habits which are difficult to correct later on.

In the Main Texts, every effort has been made to provide interesting dialogues. We have also included various aspects of Korean culture that are necessary in learning the language of Korea. In doing so, we have tried to blend cultural information into the text in a natural way, and have tried to present the Korean culture of today, avoiding a dry over-emphasis on traditional culture. The division of most lesson's Main Text into two sections is merely for a change of scene, and is not academically significant.

Explanations of grammatical items are presented in English for clearer understanding on the part of students who do not have the benefit of a teacher. The examples, however, are given without translations, and are intended to further elucidate the way in which a given grammatical item is used.

The Exercises should give students ample practice of the new vocabulary and grammatical items presented in each lesson.

6. A glossary of vocabulary and grammatical items, and English translations of the Main Texts can be found at the back of the book. In Volume 1, however, the English translations are placed immediately following each Main Text.

In Volumes 2 and 3, however, the English translation of the dialogues has been placed at the back of the book. It is the authors' view that whereas the English translation is helpful at the early stages, it can become a hindrance at more advanced levels. At these levels it should be used more as a reference: for checking comprehension, for discovering the nuance of various expressions above and beyond their "dictionary definitions," and for cultural and social insights through the many footnotes.

7. The format of the glossary of Volume 1 is different from that of the other two volumes. In Volume 1, each item is listed exactly as it appears in the text, along with page on which it can be found. We feel that the beginning student cannot be expected to know the basic forms of new words. However, as intermediate and advanced students are at a higher level, all items in the glossaries of Volumes 2 and 3 are listed by their basic forms, along with the number of the lesson in which they are introduced.

Sang-Oak Lee

일러두기

1. 본 한국어 교과서는 서울대 어학연구소 주관으로 이상억, 윤희원, 한재영, 한미선, 최은규에 의해 1(149p), 2(151p), 3(199p)의 세 권으로 집필되어 있으며, 각 권은 각각 25개의 과로 구성되어 있다.

2. 본 한국어 교과서에 담은 내용의 전반적인 방향은 다음과 같다.
   ① 우선 쉬워야 할 것.(특히 1권과 2권)
   ② 교육적이면서 재미가 있을 것.(특히 3권)
   ③ 한국어가 가지고 있는 음운, 문법 등의 특징적인 정보가 반영되도록 할 것.
   ④ 한국의 문화에 대하여 드러나지는 않되 자연스럽게 소개가 되도록 할 것.
   ⑤ 혼자서도 어느 정도 자습이 가능하도록 할 것.

3. 위의 전반적인 방향을 충족시키기 위하여 교과서에 담을 기초 어휘의 목록을 작성하였다. 그를 위하여 기존의 어휘 빈도 조사들에 의존했지만, 해당 장면의 대화에 필요한 어휘일 경우에는 기초어휘의 우선 순위에 벗어나는 어휘들일지라도 대상으로 삼았다. 문법 항목에 대해서는 먼저 국어의 문법 형태소 목록을 작성하고, 사용 비중이 높은 문법 사항을 골라서 다룰 대상으로 삼았다. 발음에 대해서는 국어에 나타나는 발음 현상과 음운 규칙들을 먼저 정리하고 해당 현상과 규칙에 부합되는 용례가 나타나는 자리에서 연습이 되도록 하였다.

4. 한국어 1권에서는 처음 다섯과를 통하여 한글을 익히도록 하였다. 특히 직접 써보는 과정을 두어 한글의 글자 구조를 익히도록 하였다.

5. 각 과는 어휘와 발음, 본문, 문법, 연습문제로 구성되어 있다. 어휘에서는 매과 새로이 소개되는 어휘에 대하여 영어로 간단한 설명을 두었다. 사전이 없이도 공부가 가능하도록 하기 위한 조처이다. 발음에서는 국어의 발음을 익히는 데에 필요한 단어들을

중심으로 다루었다. 본문은 가능한 한 재미있는 장면이 담기도록 노력하였다. 그와 함께 한국의 문화가 자연스럽게 소개될 수 있도록 대화 내용을 유도하였다. 그렇지만 한국의 문화가 과거의 것만이 아니라 현재 우리의 모습도 진정한 우리의 문화라는 점을 염두에 두어 고루한 내용이 되는 것을 피하고자 하였다. 본문은 대부분 제1부와 제2부로 구성이 되어 있는데 장면의 전환을 위한 조처로 이해하면 될 것이다. 본문을 읽어 나가면서 문제가 될 만한 항목들에 대해서는 본문의 영어 번역 부분에서 따로 영어로 설명을 베풀었다. **문법** 항목은 바로 영어로 설명하여, 자습자에 대해 배려하였다. 그러나 해당 문법항목이 나타나는 용례에 대해서는 의도적으로 번역을 달지 않았다. 주어진 문법 항목의 설명만으로는 갈증을 느끼는 자습자를 고려한 것이다. 연습문제는 주로 해당 과에서 학습한 내용을 충분히 연습할 수 있도록 하였다.

6. 각 권의 뒤에는 어휘·문법 색인과 본문의 영어 번역이 실리게 된다. 1권과는 달리 2. 3권에서는 본문의 영어 번역을 책의 맨 뒤로 돌렸다. 1권의 수준에서는 도움을 줄 수 있는 영어 번역이 2. 3권에서는 바로 보이면 방해가 될 수도 있기 때문이다.

7. 어휘·문법 색인은 1권과 2. 3권의 모습을 달리하였다. 1권에서는 본문에 나타나는 형태를 그대로 보여주며, 해당면수를 밝혔다. 기본형을 모르는 초심자를 고려한 조처이다. 2. 3권에서는 학습자의 수준을 고려하여 기본형태를 보이고, 출현 과를 밝혔다.

이 상 억

Contents

목 차

* Korean Vowel Chart

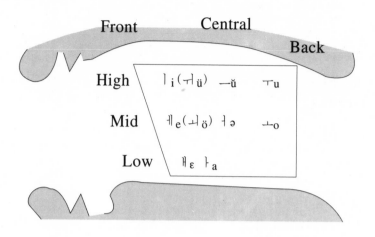

	Front	Central	Back
High	ㅣi (ㅟü)	ㅡŭ	ㅜu
Mid	ㅔe (ㅚö) ㅓə		ㅗo
Low	ㅐɛ ㅏa		

* Korean Cosonant Chart

Where does it happens? What happens?		Bilabial	Alveolar	Alveo-palatal	Velar	Glottal
Stops						
Plain	vs*	p ㅂ	t ㄷ		k ㄱ	
(intervocalic)	vd	b ㅂ	d ㄷ		g ㄱ	
Glottalized	vs	pp ㅃ	tt ㄸ		kk ㄲ	
Aspirated	vs	p' ㅍ	t' ㅌ		k' ㅋ	
Affricates						
Plain	vs			ch ㅈ		
(intervocalic)	vd			j ㅈ		
Glottalized	vs			cc ㅉ		
Aspirated	vs			ch' ㅊ		
Fricatives						
Plain	vs		s ㅅ			h ㅎ
Glottalized	vs		ss ㅆ			
Resonants						
Nasal	vd	m ㅁ	n ㄴ		ng ㅇ	
Lateral	vd		l ㄹ			
Flap	vd		r ㄹ			

제 1 과   한글(1)

1. 한글의 자모   Korean Vowels and Consonants

Han-gŭl (한글, the Korean alphabet) consists of forty letters. Twenty-one of these represent vowels (including thirteen diphthongs), and nineteen represent consonants. Twenty-four are basic, while the others are compounds of the basic letters.

Vowels :

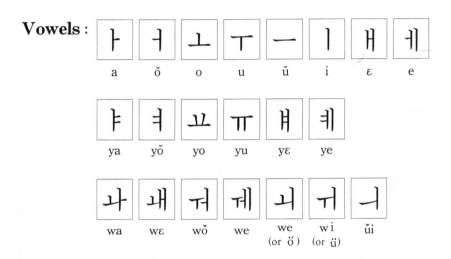

Consonants :

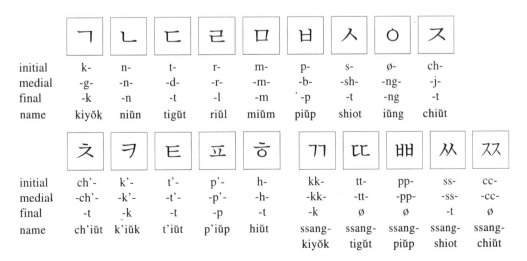

	ㄱ	ㄴ	ㄷ	ㄹ	ㅁ	ㅂ	ㅅ	ㅇ	ㅈ
initial	k-	n-	t-	r-	m-	p-	s-	ø-	ch-
medial	-g-	-n-	-d-	-r-	-m-	-b-	-sh-	-ng-	-j-
final	-k	-n	-t	-l	-m	-p	-t	-ng	-t
name	kiyŏk	niŭn	tigŭt	riŭl	miŭm	piŭp	shiot	iŭng	chiŭt

	ㅊ	ㅋ	ㅌ	ㅍ	ㅎ	ㄲ	ㄸ	ㅃ	ㅆ	ㅉ
initial	ch'-	k'-	t'-	p'-	h-	kk-	tt-	pp-	ss-	cc-
medial	-ch'-	-k'-	-t'-	-p'-	-h-	-kk-	-tt-	-pp-	-ss-	-cc-
final	-t	-k	-t	-p	-t	-k	ø	ø	-t	ø
name	ch'iŭt	k'iŭk	t'iŭt	p'iŭp	hiŭt	ssang-kiyŏk	ssang-tigŭt	ssang-piŭp	ssang-shiot	ssang-chiŭt

2. 한글 쓰기   How to write Han'gǔl

All symbols of Han'gǔl are written from top to bottom and from left to right. The order of the strokes is as illustrated below. Strokes are never interrupted, not even when they change direction halfway.

자음   Consonants

모음　　**Vowels**

	1	2	3	4	5
ㅏ	ㅣ	ㅏ			
ㅐ	ㅣ	ㅏ	ㅐ		
ㅑ	ㅣ	ㅏ	ㅑ		
ㅒ	ㅣ	ㅏ	ㅑ	ㅒ	
ㅓ	ㆍ	ㅓ			
ㅔ	ㆍ	ㅓ	ㅔ		
ㅕ	ㆍ	ㅕ	ㅕ		
ㅖ	ㆍ	ㅕ	ㅕ	ㅖ	
ㅗ	ㆍ	ㅗ			
ㅘ	ㆍ	ㅗ	ㅘ	ㅘ	
ㅙ	ㆍ	ㅗ	ㅘ	ㅘ	ㅙ

	1	2	3	4	5
ㅚ	ㆍ	ㅗ	ㅚ		
ㅛ	ㆍ	ㅛ	ㅛ		
ㅜ	ㅜ	ㅜ			
ㅝ	ㅜ	ㅜ	ㅝ		
ㅞ	ㅜ	ㅜ	ㅝ	ㅞ	
ㅟ	ㅜ	ㅜ	ㅟ		
ㅠ	ㅜ	ㅠ	ㅠ		
ㅡ	ㅡ	ㅡ			
ㅢ	ㅡ	ㅢ			
ㅣ	ㅣ				

3. 쓰기 연습 Let's write.

ㅏ	ㅏ	ㅏ							
ㅑ	ㅑ	ㅑ							
ㅓ	ㅓ	ㅓ							
ㅕ	ㅕ	ㅕ							
ㅗ	ㅗ								
ㅛ	ㅛ								
ㅜ	ㅜ								
ㅠ	ㅠ								
ㅡ	ㅡ								
ㅣ	ㅣ								
ㅐ	ㅐ	ㅐ							
ㅔ	ㅔ								
ㅚ	ㅚ								
ㅓ	ㅓ								

ㄱ	ㄱ								
ㄴ	ㄴ								
ㄷ	ㄷ								
ㄹ	ㄹ								
ㅁ	ㅁ								
ㅂ	ㅂ								
ㅅ	ㅅ								
ㅇ	ㅇ								
ㅈ	ㅈ								
ㅊ	ㅊ								
ㅋ	ㅋ								
ㅌ	ㅌ								
ㅍ	ㅍ								
ㅎ	ㅎ								

제 2 과　한글(2)

1. 소리 듣고 따라 읽기　Listen and repeat.

ㅇ

이	아	어
으	오	우

ㄱ

기	가	거
그	고	구

ㄴ

니	나	너
느	노	누

ㄷ

디	다	더
드	도	두

ㅁ

미	마	머
므	모	무

ㅅ

시	사	서
스	소	수

Iung 'ㅇ', preceding vowels, is phonetically of no value (example : 아 [a]. Only the one followin vowels within a syllable has phonetis value (e.g. : 강[kaŋ])

이	아	어	으	오	우	기	가	거	그	고
구	시	사	서	스	소	수	히	하	허	흐

2. 읽기 연습　　Let's read.

소
bull

무
radish

구두
shoes

아기
baby

오이
cucumber

하마
hippopotamus

호수 lake

바다 sea

고기 fish

나무 tree
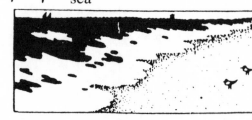

3. 읽기와 쓰기 연습   Let's read and write.

나			

너			

소			

무			

구두			

아기			

오이			

하마			

호수			

바다			

고기			

나무			

4. 쓰기 연습　　Let's write.

구	느	노	누	다	더	드	도	두	미	마
므	머	시	사	서	히	하	허	흐	허	후

5. 모음의 형성　Formation of some vowels and diphthongs

ㅐ ＝ ㅏ ＋ ㅣ [ɛ]　　ㅚ ＝ ㅗ ＋ ㅣ [we] or [ö]

ㅒ ＝ ㅑ ＋ ㅣ [yɛ]　　ㅘ ＝ ㅗ ＋ ㅏ [wa]

ㅔ ＝ ㅓ ＋ ㅣ [e]　　ㅙ ＝ ㅗ ＋ ㅐ [wɛ]

ㅖ ＝ ㅕ ＋ ㅣ [ye]　　ㅝ ＝ ㅜ ＋ ㅓ [wŏ]

ㅢ ＝ ＿ ＋ ㅣ [ŭi]　　ㅞ ＝ ㅜ ＋ ㅔ [we]

ㅟ ＝ ㅜ ＋ ㅣ [wi] or [ü]

The distinction between ㅐ and ㅔ-has been lost among ghe youger generation below 50 of age in casual Korean speech.

As a result of loss of distinction between ㅐ and ㅔ, the three vowels ㅙ, ㅞ and ㅚ are not normally distinguished in Standard Korean speech today. They all end up with [we] also.

The distinction between ㅒ and ㅖ has also been lost among the youger generation and ㅖ may be pronounced as ㅔ after consonants except ㄹ.

시계 [시계｜시게]　　지폐 [지폐｜지페]　　except 실례 [실례]

ㅢ at the syllable-initial position without any preceding consonant may be pronounced as ＿ : 의사 [의사｜으사]. ㅢ at the non-initjal position of a syllable or at the syllable-initial position with a preceding consonant, ㅢ may be pronounced as ㅣ : 회의 [회의｜회이]. When ㅢ is used as possessive particle, it may be pronounced as ㅔ : 우리의 [우리의｜우리에], 의의의 [으이에]

ㅚ and ㅟ are rarely pronouced as simple vowels (i.e. as [o] and [u])in Standard Korean. Therefore, those are put together with diphthongs. They are more often pronounced as diphthongs. i.e., as[we] and [wi] respectively.

제 3 과 한글(3)

1. 소리 듣고 따라 읽기 Listen and repeat.

O					
	이	아	어	야	여
	으	오	우	요	유

ㄱ					
	기	가	거	갸	겨
	그	고	구	교	규

ㄴ					
	니	나	너	냐	녀
	느	노	누	뇨	뉴

ㄷ					
	디	다	더	댜	뎌
	드	도	두	됴	듀

ㅁ					
	미	마	머	먀	며
	므	모	무	묘	뮤

ㅅ					
	시	사	서	샤	셔
	스	소	수	쇼	슈

ㅎ	히	하	허	햐	혀
	흐	호	후	효	휴

1-1. 빈 칸 메우기   Fill in the blanks.

ㄹ					

ㅂ					

ㅈ					

ㅊ					

ㅋ					

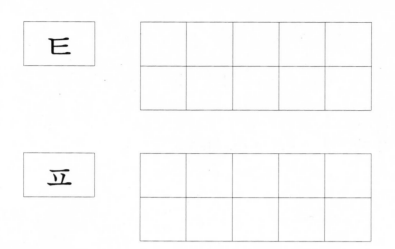

ㅌ					

ㅍ					

1−2. 쓰기 연습   Let's write.

야	겨	교	규	냐	녀	뇨	뉴	랴	려	료

2. 읽기 연습　　Let's read.

오리
duck
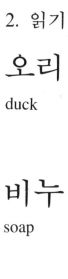

우유
milk

비누
soap
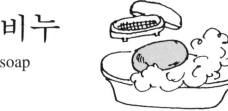

다리
bridge

머리
head

나비
butterfly

바지
trousers
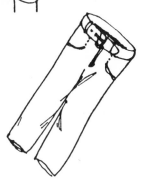

기차
train

우표
stamp

모자
hat

다리미
iron

바나나
banana

3. 읽기와 쓰기 연습   Let's read and write.

오리			

우유			

비누			

다리			

머리			

나비			

바지			

기차			

우표			

모자			

다리미			

바나나			

제 4 과 한글(4)

1. 소리 듣고 따라 읽기   Listen and repeat.

1)	가	갸	거	겨	고	교	구	규	그	기
2)	나	냐	너	녀	노	뇨	누	뉴	느	니
3)	다	댜	더	뎌	도	됴	두	듀	드	디
4)	라	랴	러	려	로	료	루	류	르	리
5)	마	먀	머	며	모	묘	무	뮤	므	미
6)	바	뱌	버	벼	보	뵤	부	뷰	브	비
7)	사	샤	서	셔	소	쇼	수	슈	스	시
8)	아	야	어	여	오	요	우	유	으	이
9)	자	쟈	저	져	조	죠	주	쥬	즈	지
10)	차	챠	처	쳐	초	쵸	추	츄	츠	치
11)	카	캬	커	켜	코	쿄	쿠	큐	크	키
12)	타	탸	터	텨	토	툐	투	튜	트	티
13)	파	퍄	퍼	펴	포	표	푸	퓨	프	피
14)	하	햐	허	혀	호	효	후	휴	흐	히

* Order of Vowels and Consonants

1) Vowels

ㅏ ㅑ ㅓ ㅕ ㅗ ㅛ ㅜ ㅠ ㅡ ㅣ

2) Consonants

ㄱ ㄴ ㄷ ㄹ ㅁ ㅂ ㅅ

ㅇ ㅈ ㅊ ㅋ ㅌ ㅍ ㅎ

가	갸		겨		교	구	규	그	
	냐		녀	노	뇨		뉴	느	니
다	댜	더	뎌		됴	두	듀	드	
	랴		려	로		루	류		리
마	먀	머		모	묘		뮤	므	
바	뱌		벼		뵤		뷰	브	비
	샤		셔	소	쇼	수	슈	스	
아		어	여		요			으	이
자	쟈		져	조	죠		쥬	즈	지
	챠	처	쳐		쵸		츄	츠	
	캬		켜	코	쿄	쿠	큐		키
타	탸	터	텨	토	툐		튜	트	티
	파	퍼	펴		표	푸	퓨	프	
하	햐		혀	호		후		흐	히

2. 읽기 연습   Let's read.

자 — measure

차 — car

야구 — baseball

보리 — barley

커피 — coffee

포도 — grape

여우 — fox

카드 — card

휴지 — tissue

사자 — lion

토마토 — tomato

피아노 — piano

3. 읽기와 쓰기 연습   Let's read and write.

자			

차			

야구			

보리			

커피			

포도			

여우			

카드			

휴지			

사자			

토마토			

피아노			

4. 쓰기 연습　　Let's write.

더	도	디	버	부	비	저	조	주	초	치

뎌	됴	드	벼	뷰	브	져	죠	쥬	쵸	츠

제 5 과 한글(5)

1. 글자를 모아 쓰기 How to compose syllabic units.

When we write individual letters in a syllabic unit for actual writing, there are five cases. As illustrated in the following diagram, the individual letters are arranged and proportioned to fit neatly into a square box, and are always read from left to right, then top to bottom.

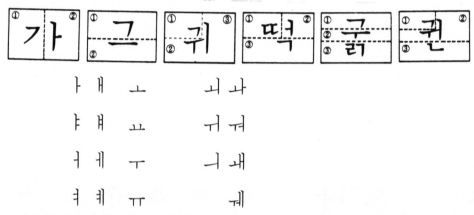

ㅏ ㅐ   ㅗ   ㅚ ㅘ

ㅑ ㅒ   ㅛ   ㅝ ㅟ

ㅓ ㅔ   ㅜ   ㅢ ㅙ

ㅕ ㅖ   ㅠ   ㅞ

A maximal Korean syllable structure is CVCC, where C represents "consonant" and V "vowel". While C is optional, V is obligatory. The Korean syllable structure can therefore be re-written as (C) V (C) (C). All the possible combinations of the syllable occurrences are exemplified as the following :

$$V : 아, 와, 왜 \qquad CV : 가, 보, 뛰$$
$$CVC : 낙, 불, 꽝, \qquad VC : 얼, 움, 은$$
$$VCC : 않, 없, 읊 \qquad CVCC : 값, 못, 덟$$

When the syllable structure of Korean is typically CVC (Consonant-Vowel-Consonant) ; in initial position of the Korean syllable 'ㄱ' is pronounced as [k] as in '거리', in intervocalic position (or between vowels) it is voiced as [g] as in '아가', in final position it is unreleased as [k˺] as in '각'.

1-1. 받침의 발음 Pronunciation of syllable-final consonants

Twenty-seven forms of final consonant(s) in Korean are pronounced as only seven sounds as follows :

ㄱ, ㅋ, ㄲ, ㄳ, ㄺ as 〔ㄱ〕

ㄴ, ㄵ, ㄶ as 〔ㄴ〕

ㄷ. ㅅ, ㅈ, ㅊ, ㅌ, ㅎ, ㅆ as 〔ㄷ〕

ㄹ, ㄼ, ㄽ, ㄾ, ㅀ as 〔ㄹ〕 (in 넓-, and 밟-, either ㄹ, ㅂ is
    pronounced)

ㅁ, ㄻ as 〔ㅁ〕

ㅂ, ㅍ, ㅄ, ㄿ as 〔ㅂ〕

ㅇ as 〔ㅇ〕

1-2. 소리 듣고 따라 읽기 Listen and repeat.

각

간	갇	갈
감	갑	강

묵

왁

꼭

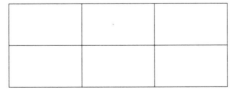

떡

쉭

박

죽

턱

혹

2. 소리 듣고 따라 읽기 Listen and repeat.

애		에	애	와
		위	위	의

개				

배				

eye

눈		

mouth

입		

star

별		

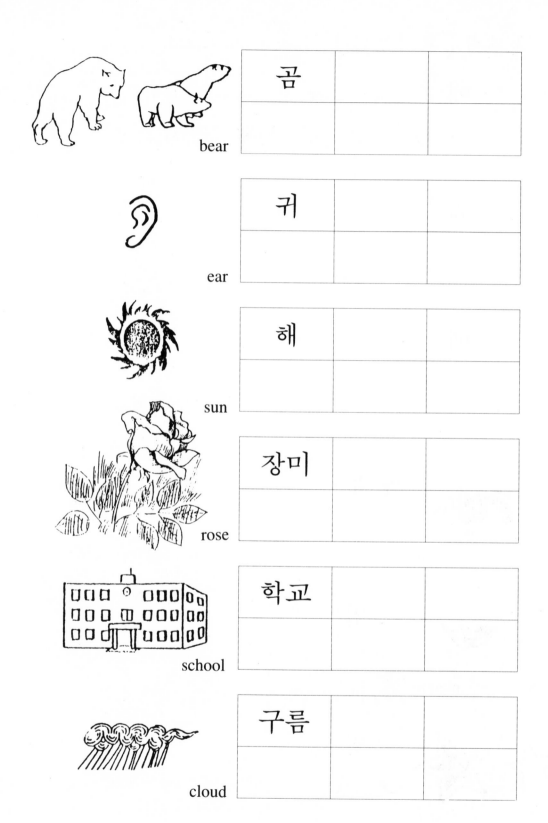

곰		

bear

귀		

ear

해		

sun

장미		

rose

학교		

school

구름		

cloud

3. 쓰기 연습   Let's write.

안	녕	하	세	요	정	말	반	가	워	요

제 6 과   안녕

Lesson 6   Hi !

※ 어휘   Vocabulary

안녕	peacefulness	계시다	to be, stay
안녕하다	to be peaceful	또	again
안녕히	in peace	만나다	to meet
가다	to go		

* The form 안녕하다. mostly used in dictionaries is listed.

☎ 발음   Pronunciation

1. When two 'ㄴ's are pronounced in a row, say each syllable separately, distinguishing clearly tetween them : 안녕 [안│녕]
2. 만나다 [만│나다]

A. 안녕!   Hi!

B. 안녕!   Hi!

A. 안녕하세요?   Hello.

B. 안녕하세요?   Hello.

A. 안녕히 가세요. Good-bye.

B. 안녕히 가세요. Good-bye.

A. 또 만나요.   See you again.

B. 또 만나요.   See you again.

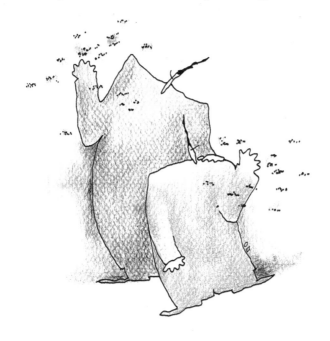

☞ 문법 Grammar

1. -요.

    (1) '-요' is a polite, informal verb ending.

    (2) Both questions and statements can end with '-요' in Korean. They are differentiated only by intonation.

    (3) A verb can be a complete sentence in Korean.

가│요?(↗)	Do (you) go?
가│요.(↘)	(I) go.
만나│요?	Do (you) meet (him)?
만나│요?	(I) meet (him).

2. -세요?

    (1) '세요?' is more polite than '-요?'. It implies respect of the speaker for the subject of the verb.

    (2) The answer to '-세요?' is not '-세요?' but '-요' when referring to the first person.

가│세요?	Do you go?
가│요.	I go.
만나│세요?	Do you meet (him)?
만나│요?	I meet (him).

3. -세요.

    (1) '세요' means 'Please do -' when referring to the second person.

    (2) When referring to the third person, '-세요' is just a polite ending.

가│세요.	please go?
가│요.	(He) goes.
만나│세요.	Please meet (him).
만나│요.	(She) meets (him).

4. Unlike in English, there are two basically different ways to say 'Good-bye!' depending on the situation. To say good-bye, one does not say "안녕하세요", but rather "안녕히 가세요" or "안녕히 계세요", depending on whether the other person is leaving or staying.

   (1) If the speakers leave the place at the same time, both of them say "안녕히 가세요".

   (2) If one of the speakers stays in the place, those who are leaving say "안녕히 계세요" to the person who will stay.

5. "안녕!" is used among children.

   "안녕하세요." is a common style among adults.

▨ 연습   Practice

1. Fill in the blanks.

   (1) (When both of the speakers leave the place at the same time)

   Good-bye!   안녕히 |_____

   Good-bye!   안녕히 |_____

   (2) A is leaving, B is staying.

   A : Good-bye!   안녕히 |_____

   B : Good-bye!   안녕히 |_____

2. Translate into Korean.

   (1) Do you go (there) again?

   (2)   I go (there) again.

   (3) Do you meet (her) again?

   (4)   I meet (her) again.

제 7 과　좋아요?

Lesson 7　Is (it) good?

※ 어휘　Vocabulary

좋다	to be good	비싸다	to be expensive
네	yes	싸다	to be inexpensive
이것	this (thing)	아니오	no
-도	also, too	칠	7
저것	that thing over there	천	1,000
다	all, both	그것	that (thing)
얼마	how much	-예요?	Is it - ?
만	10,000	-예요.	It is - .
원	won (Korean monetary unit)		

A. 좋아요?	Is it good?
B. 네, 좋아요.	Yes, it is good.
A. 이것도 좋아요?	Is this also good?
B. 네, 그것도 좋아요.	Yes, that is also good.
A. 저것도 좋아요?	Is that also good?
B. 네, 저것도 좋아요.	Yes, that is also good.
A. 다 좋아요?	Are they all good?
B. 다 좋아요.	They are all good.

* * * * * * * * *

A. 얼마예요?	How much is it?
B. 만원이에요.	It is 10,000 won.
A. 비싸요.	It is expensive.
B. 비싸요?	Expensive?
A. 이것도 비싸요?	Is this also expensive?
B. 아니오, 싸요.	No, it is not expensive.
A. 얼마예요?	How much is it?
B. 칠천원이에요.	It is 7,000 won.

1. 'ㅎ' is not pronounced when the following syllable begins with a vowel : 좋아요[조아요]

2. **When the following syllable begins with ㄱ, ㄷ, ㅂ, ㅈ, the consonant following 'ㅎ' is aspirated : 좋다[조타]**

3. The pronunciation of the final consonant in a syllable is realized as the first consonant of the following syllable which begins with a vowel : 만원이에요[마눠니에요]

☞ 문법   Grammar

1. -예요?

  (1) '-예요?' following a noun means 'Is it -?'
  (2) '-예요?' is used when the noun to which it is attached ends with a vowel.

6과│예요?	Is it│ Lesson 6?
대화│예요?	Is it│ a dialogue?
사과│예요?	Is it│ an apple?

2. -이에요?

  (1) '-이에요?' and '-예요?' have exactly the same meaning.
  (2) '-이에요?' follows nouns ending with a consonant.

만원│이에요?	Is it│ 10,000 won?
선물│이에요?	Is it│ a present?
연습│이에요?	Is it│ a practice?

  * In English, there are two different 'to be's, one meaning "to exist" and the other meaning "to be equal to". '-예요/-이에요' means "to be equal to".

  * When '-예요/-이에요' endings are not pronounced with rising intonation, they represent not questions but statements.

3. -도   also, too

이것도 아주 비싸요.　　　　　This, too, is very expensive.

4. There are two kinds of cardinal numbers : pure Korean numbers and Sino-Korean numbers which are the numbers of Chinese origin. Here are Sino Korean numbers.

0	영	10	십	20	이십	10,000	만
1	일	11	십일	30	삼십	100,000	십만
2	이	12	십이	40	사십	1,000,000	백만
3	삼	13	십삼	50	오십	10,000,000	천만
4	사	14	십사	60	육십	100,000,000	억
5	오	15	십오	70	칠십	1,000,000,000	십억
6	육	16	십육	80	팔십	10,000,000,000	백억
7	칠	17	십칠	90	구십	100,000,000,000	천억
8	팔	18	십팔	100	백	1,000,000,000,000	조
9	구	19	십구	1,000	천		

▨ 연습　Practice

1. Fill in the blanks.
   (1) Is this | good?　　　　　이것 |--------------
       　　　　| cheap?　　　　　　　|--------------
       　　　　| expensive?　　　　　|--------------

   (2) That is | an apple.　　　　저것|--------------
       　　　　| 1,000 won.　　　　　|--------------
       　　　　| very expensive.　　|--------------

2. Translate into Korean.
   (1) It is good.
   (2) It is expensive.
   (3) It is cheap.
   (4) How much is it?
   (5) It is 1,000 won.

제 8 과　여기가 어디예요?

Lesson 8　Where are we?

※ 어휘　Vocabulary

여기	here	얼마나	how long
-가	(subject market)	걸리다	to take(time)
어디	where	오	five
종로	(a major street in Seoul)	분	mintue
대사관	embassy	고맙습니다.	Thank you.
저쪽	that way	몇	how many
멀다	to be far	광화문	Kwanghwa-mun
가깝다	to be near		

A. 여기가 어디예요?　　　Where are we?
B. 종로예요.　　　We are in Chong-No.

A. 대사관이 어디예요?　　　Where is the embassy?
B. 저쪽이에요.　　　It is over there.

A. 멀어요?　　　Is it far?
B. 아니오, 가까워요.　　　No. It is nearby.

A. 얼마나 걸려요?　　　How long does it take?
B. 오 분 걸려요.　　　It takes 5 minutes.

* * * * * * * * *

A. 대사관이 멀어요?　　　Is the embassy far?
B. 네, 멀어요.　　　Yes, it is far.

A. 몇 분 걸려요?　　　How many minutes does it take?
B. 40 (사십) 분 걸려요.　　　It takes 40 minutes.

A. 어디예요?　　　Where is it?
B. 광화문이에요.　　　It is in Kwanghwa-Mun.

A. 고맙습니다.　　　Thank you.
B. 안녕히 가세요.　　　Bye!

☎ 발음　Pronunciation

1. '초' as the final consonant of a syllable is not pronounced as '초' but as 'ㄷ' when the following syllable begins with a consonant : 몇 분 [멷분] ➞ [며뿐]

2. Two consecutive 'ㄹ's sound like [l], but the tip of the tongue should touch the roof of the mouth, rather than the front teeth : 걸려요 [걸려요]

☞ 문법　Grammar

1. –예요.

* '예요?' in '어디예요?' is nothing but the abbreviated from of '~이에요?' after mouns ending with a vowels including '이'.

　　어디예요?　　　　　Where is it?
　　영이에요?　　　　　Are you Young-i

2. –가

(1) '–가'marks the subject of a verb or descriptive verb. It is often omitted in conversation, and can be replaced with a short pause.

(2) '–가' follows nouns which end with a vowel.

　　학교가 멀어요?　　　Is the school far?
　　학교가 멀어요.　　　The school is far.

　　가게가 가까워요?　　Is the shop nearby?
　　가게가 가까워요.　　The shop is nearby.

3. –이

(1) The meaning of '–이' is exactly the same as '–가'.

(2) '–이' follows nouns which end with a consonant.

　　그 집이 좋아요?　　　Is that house good?
　　그 집이 좋아요.　　　That house is good.

　　옷이 싸요?　　　　　Are the clothes cheap?
　　옷이 싸요.　　　　　The clothes are cheap.

4. -이
   (1) Subject markers arc optional in conversation.
   (2) Subject markers can be replaced with a short pause.

멀어요.	It is far
아주 멀어요.	It is very far
대사관이 멀어요.	The embassy is far.
대사관이 아주 멀어요.	The embassy is very far.

5. 가깝다   is near

   '이' at the stem-fiual position of '가깝-' is changed into '우' before '- ㅓ요.'

가까워요.	It is near.

▨ 연습   Practice

1. Fill in the proper subject marker.
   (1) 여기(   )   어디예요?
   (2) 대사관(   )   멀어요?
   (3) 집(   )   가까워요?
   (4) 사과(   )   비싸요?
   (5) 옷(   )   싸요?

2. Read the numbers.
   (1) 135
   (2) 2,468
   (3) 70,101
   (4) 901,120
   (5) 1,020,301

3. Translate into Korean.
   (1) Where are we?
   (2) Where is it?
   (3) How long does it take?
   (4) It takes 10 minutes.
   (5) Thank you.

제 9 과   누구세요?

Lesson 9   Who is it?

❋ 어휘   Vocabulary

누구	who	어서	please, quickly
저	I, me (humble)	반갑다	to be glad to see
아	Ah	앉다	to sit
들어오다	to come in	커피	coffee
안녕하세요.	Hello.	들다	to eat (polite)
친구	friend	설탕	sugar
같이	together	한	one
오다	to come	개	piece

* 어서 is used only in commands.

☎ 발음   Pronunciation

1. 넣다 [너타] : 넣으세요 [너으세요]
2. 앉다 [안따] : 앉으세요 [안즈세요]
3. 'ㅌ' in front of '이' is pronounced as 'ㅊ' : 같이 [가치]

-42-

A. 누구세요?	Who is it?
B. 저예요.	It's me.

A. 누구요?	Who?
B. 혜선이에요.	Hye-Sun.

A. 아, 네, 들어오세요.	Oh, yes, come in.
B. 안녕하세요?	How are you?

A. 네, 안녕하세요?	Fine, and you?
B. 친구도 같이 왔어요.	I've come here with my friend.

* * * * * * * * *

A. 어서 오세요.	Come on in.
B. 반갑습니다.	Nice to see you.

A. 앉으세요.	Have a seat.
B. 고맙습니다.	Thank you.

A. 커피 드시겠어요?	Would you like some coffee?
B. 네, 고맙습니다.	Yes, thank you.

A. 설탕 넣으세요?	Do you take sugar?
B. 네, 한 개요.	Yes, one spoon, please.

☞ 문법 Grammar

1. -세요. (cf.p.32)

    (1) '-세요.' is an honorific imperative ending.

    (2) '-세요.' follows verb roots ending with a vowel.

    (3) '어서 오세요.' is often used as a greeting to customers in stores and restaurants.

    (4) '-셔요.' may be used in place of '-세요.'

오ㅣ세요.	Come (here), please.
들어오ㅣ세요.	Come in, please.
어서 오ㅣ세요.	Come on in, please.

2. -으세요.

    (1) '-으세요.' is the same as '-세요.' in its meaning.

    (2) '-으세요.' follows verb roots ending with a consonant.

    (3) '-으셔요' may be used in place of '-으세요.'

넣ㅣ으세요.	Put (it) in, please.
앉ㅣ으세요.	Have a seat, please.
읽ㅣ으세요.	Read (it), please.

3. 같이[가치] together

오세요.	Come (here), please.
같이 오세요.	Come (here) together, please.
친구도 같이 오세요.	Come (here) with (your) friend, please.

4. 누구 who

누구세요?	Who is it? (polite)
누구예요?	Who is it? (informal)
누구요?	who?(asking for a repetition of a name; '-요?' is attacked directly to '누구'. This ending may directry follow pronouns or nouns.)

1. Fill in the blanks.

    (1) Please | come in.   들어오 |-------------

             | go.   가 |-------------

             | meet(him).   만나 |-------------

    (2) Please | sit down.   앉 |-------------

             | wear(it).   입 |-------------

             | close(it).   닫 |-------------

2. Translate into Korean.

    (1) Who is it?

    (2) It's me.

    (3) Nice to see you.

    (4) Come on in, please.

    (5) Would you like some coffee?

Cardinal numbers			Ordinal numbers		
Sino-Korean numbers	Modifier	Pure-Korean numbers	(Date)		
1 일	한	하나 one	첫째	하루	the first(day)
2 이	두	둘 two	둘째	이틀	the second(day)
3 삼	세, 석, 서	셋 three	셋째	사흘	the third(day)
4 사	네, 넉, 너	넷 four	넷째	나흘	the fourth(day)
5 오	다섯, 다	다섯 five	다섯째	닷새	the fifth(day)
6 육(륙)	여섯, 엿	여섯 six	여섯째	엿새	the sixth(day)
7 칠	일곱	일곱 seven	일곱째	이레	the sevebth(day)
8 팔	여덟	여덟 eight	여덟째	여드레	the eight(day)
9 구	아홉	아홉 nine	아홉째	아흐레	the ninth(day)
10 십	열	열 ten	열째	열흘	the tenth(day)

제 10 과   신문 주세요.

Lesson 10   Give me a newspaper.

❀ 어휘   Vocabulary

신문	newspaper	사전	dictionary
주다	to give	-은	(topic marker)
어느	which	-에	at (a time or place)
있다	to be (exist)	저쪽	over there
얼마	how much	잡지	magazine
삼	three	없다	not to exist
백	hundred		(opposite of 있다)

☎ 발음   Pronunciation

1. 'ㅄ' in front of consonants is pronounced as 'ㅂ' : 없다 [업:따]
2. In front of vowels 'ㅄ' is pronounced as follows : 없어요[업써요]

A. 신문 주세요.   Give me a newspaper, please.
B. 어느 신문이오?   Which newspaper?

A. 한국일보요.   The Korea Times, please.
B. 여기 있어요.   Here you are.

A. 얼마예요?   How much is it?
B. 300(삼백) 원이에요.   It is 300 won.

A. 여기 있어요.   Here you are.
B. 안녕히 가세요.   Bye!

* * * * * * * * *

A. 사전은 어디 있어요?   Where are the dictionaries?
B. 저쪽에 있어요.   They are over there.

A. 잡지도 있어요?   Are there magazines, also?
B. 네, 있어요.   Yes, there are.

A. 신문은 어디 있어요?   Where are the newspapers?
B. 신문은 여기 있어요.   Here are the newspapers.

A. 뉴욕 타임즈 없어요?   Don't you have the New York
                        Times?
B. 뉴욕 타임즈 없어요.   I don't have the New York Times.

☞ 문법   Grammar

1. -어요.

   (1) '-어요' is a polite, informal ending(c.f. pp.52, 68).

   (2) '-어요' follows syllables containing the vowels '어' '여' '우'
   '유' '으' '이'('Yin' or dark vowels).

   있ㅣ어요?   Do you have (it)?
   있ㅣ어요.   I have (it).

   없ㅣ어요?   Don't you have (it)?
   없ㅣ어요.   I don't have (it).

2. -이오

   (1) '-이오?' is a polite ending meaning "You are talking about-?

   (2) '-이오' is used when asking for or giving confirmation or
   repetition

   (3) '-이오' follows nouns which end with a consonant.

   그 사람ㅣ이오? You are talking about him?
   그 사람ㅣ이오. I am talking about him.

   이 책ㅣ이오? You mean this book?
   이 책ㅣ이오 I mean that book.

3. -은

   (1) '-은' is used for emphasizing a subject or an object. It also
   marks the general topic of the sentence.

   (2) '-은' follows syllables that end with a consonant.

   없어요.   There isn't.
   신문 없어요.   I don't have a newspaper.
   신문은 없어요.   I don't have a newspaper
                       (but I might have something else).
   여기 신문은 없어요. There aren't any newspapers here
                       (but there might be some other things).

-48-

☒ 연습   Practice

1. Fill in the blanks.

    (1) Do you have| a newspaper?   신문 |_____

          I have| a newspaper.   신문 |_____

    (2) You mean| a dictionary?   사전 |_____

          I mean| a dictionary.   사전 |_____

2. Translate into Korean.

    (1) Give me an apple.

    (2) Here you are.

    (3) How much (is it)?

    (4) I have (it).

    (5) I don't have (it).

제 11 과　김치 맛있어요?

Lesson 11　Does kimchi taste good?

❀ 어휘　Vocabulary

김치	kimchi	괜찮아요	(It) is O.K.
맛있다	to taste good	어때요?	How is (it)?
좋다	to be good	나쁘다	to be bad
맛	taste	나빠요	(It) is bad

☎ 발음　Pronunciation

1. '씨' is pronounced 'ㄷ' before a consonant :
   맛있다 [마싣다] → [마시따]

2. '맛없다' is an exception : 맛없다[마덥따], 맛없어요[마덥써요]

A. 김치 맛있어요? Is kimchi delicious?
B. 네, 맛있어요. Yes, it is delicious.

A. 이것도 맛있어요? Is this also good?
B. 이것도 맛있어요. This is also good.

A. 저것은 어때요? What about that one?
B. 저것은 맛없어요. That doesn't taste good.

A. 맛없어요? It doesn't taste good?
B. 네, 맛없어요. No, it doesn't taste good.

* * * * * * * *

A. 이것 괜찮아요? Is this O. K. ?
B. 네, 괜찮아요. Yes, it's O. K.

A. 이것은 어때요? What about this, then?
B. 그것은 나빠요. That is bad.

A. 저것은 어때요? How about that one, then?
B. 저것은 괜찮아요. That one is O. K.

A. 괜찮아요? It's O. K. ?
B. 네, 괜찮아요. Yes, it's O. K.

☞ 문법 Grammar

1. -어요.(cf. p. 48)

맛있ㅣ어요?	Does (it) taste good?
맛있ㅣ어요.	(It) tastes good.
맛없ㅣ어요?	Doesn't (it) taste good?
맛없ㅣ어요.	(It) doesn't taste good.

2. -아요.
   (1) The meaning of '-아요.' is the same as '-어요.'
   (2) '-아요' follows syllables containing the vowels '아' '야' '오' '요'('Yang' or bright vowels).

좋ㅣ아요?	Is (it) good?
좋ㅣ아요.	(It) is good.
많ㅣ아요?	Are there a lot?
많ㅣ아요.	There are a lot.

3. -는
   (1) '-는' is used for emphasing a subject or an object.
   (2) '-는' follows syllables that end with a vowel(cf. p. 48).

맛있어요.	(It) tastes good.
참 맛있어요.	(It) tastes very good.
사과 참 맛있어요.	The apple tastes very good.
사과는 참 맛있어요.	The apple tastes very good.

▨ 연습 Practice

1. Choose the proper ending.

   (1) Do you ㅣ eat (it)?   먹 ㅣ_____

        I ㅣ eat (it).   먹 ㅣ_____

   (2) Do you ㅣ get the phone? 전화 받 ㅣ_____

        I ㅣ get the phone.   전화 받 ㅣ_____

2. Fill in the proper topic marker ('은' or '는').
   (1) 이것( ) 어때요?
      그것( ) 맛없어요.
   (2) 사과( ) 맛있어요?
      사과( ) 괜찮아요.

3. Say the opposite words.
   (1) 싸요.
   (2) 좋아요.
   (3) 멀어요.
   (4) 없어요.
   (5) 맛있어요.

제 12 과 어디 가세요?

Lesson 12 Where are you going?

※ 어휘 Vocabulary

학교	school
-에	to (a place)
수업	class
-이	(subject marker)
몇	what, how many
시	o'clock
했다	did
벌써	already
아홉	9 (pure Korean number)
열	10(pure Korean number)
반	half
빨리	quickly
시작하다	to begin
언제	when
분	minute
-전에	before (time)
과	and
재미있다	to be interesting

☎ 발음 Pronunciation

1. 했다 [핻다] → [해따]
2. 했어요 [해써요]

A. 어디 가세요?	Where are you going?
B. 학교에 가요.	I'm going to school.
A. 수업이 있어요?	Do you have class?
B. 네, 수업이 있어요.	Yes, I have a class.
A. 몇 시에 시작해요?	What time does it begin?
B. 10 (열)시에 시작해요.	It begins at 10 o'clock.
A. 벌써 9 (아홉)시 반이에요.	It is already 9:30
빨리 가세요.	Hurry up!

* * * * * * * * *

A. 수업 시작했어요?	Has the class begun?
B. 네, 시작했어요.	Yes, it's begun.
A. 언제 시작했어요?	When did it begin?
B. 오 분 전에 시작했어요.	It began 5 minutes ago.
A. 몇 과 공부해요?	Which lesson do we study?
B. 팔 과 공부해요.	We study Lesson 8.
A. 재미있어요?	Is it interesting?
B. 네, 재미있어요.	Yes, it is interesting.

☞ 문법   Grammar

1. -해요?   Do you - ?

뭐 공부|해요?　　　　　What do you study?
한국어 공부|해요.　　　　I study Korean.

언제 시작|해요?　　　　When does it begin?
한 시에 시작|해요.　　　It begins at 1 o'clock.

2. -했어요?.   Did you - ?

공부|했어요?　　　　　Did (you) study?
공부|했어요.　　　　　(I) studied.

일|했어요?　　　　　　Did (you) work?
일|했어요.　　　　　　I worked.

3. -에   to (a place)

가세요?　　　Do you go?
학교   가세요?　　　Do you go to school?

학교에 가세요?　　　Do you go to school?
오늘 학교에 가세요?　　　Do you go to school today?

4. (1) There are two kinds of cardinal numbers in Korean.
   (2) When referring to the hour, pure Korean numbers are used.
   (3) When referring to the minute, Sino-Korean cardinal numbers are used.

1 : 00	한 시	8:00	여덟 시 〔여덜 씨〕
2 : 00	두 시	9:00	아홉 시
3 : 00	세 시	10:00	열 시
4 : 00	네 시	11:00	열한 시
5 : 00	다섯 시	12:00	열두 시
6 : 00	여섯 시	1:01	한 시 일 분
7 : 00	일곱 시	10:10	열 시 십 분

11:11 열한 시 십일 분   12:30 열두 시 삼십 분
12:12 열두 시 십이 분   (열두 시 반)

▨ 연습 Practice

1. Fill in the blanks.

   (1) Did you | make a phone call?   전화 |--------------
        I | made a phone call.   전화 |--------------

   (2) Did you | say?   말 |--------------
        I | said.   말 |--------------

2. Read the time.
   (1)   5 : 15
   (2) 11 : 37
   (3)   2 : 46
   (4)   4 : 51
   (5) 10 : 30

제 13과   어디가 아파요?

Lesson 13   Where does it hurt?

❋ 어휘   Vocabulary

아프다	to be sick, to hurt	감기	a cold
아파요	I am sick, It hurts.	걸리다	to catch (a cold)
머리	head	걸렸다	to have caught (a cold)
자주	often	걸렸어요	I've caught (a cold).
가끔	every once in a while	아직	(not) yet, still
왜	why	안	not
모르다	to not know	갔다	(I) went
몰라요	(I) don't know.	갔어요	(I) went.

☎ 발음   Pronunciation

1. 'ㄱ' after 'ㅁ' is pronounced like 'g' : 감기
2. 몇 분[멷분] → [며뿐]

A. 아파요?   Are you in pain?

B. 네, 아파요.   Yes, I'm sick.

A. 어디가 아파요?   Where does it hurt?

B. 머리가 아파요.   I have a headache.

A. 자주 아파요?   Does it hurt often?

B. 가끔 아파요.   It hurts from time to time.

A. 왜 아파요?   Why does it hurt?

B. 몰라요.   I don't know.

* * * * * * * * *

A. 어디 아파요?   Are you in pain?

B. 네, 감기 걸렸어요.   Yes, I've caught a cold.

A. 병원에 갔어요?   Did you go to a hospital?

B. 아직 안 갔어요.   Not yet.

A. 병원이 가까워요?   Is the hospital near?

B. 네, 가까워요.   Yes, it is near.

A. 몇 분쯤 걸려요?   How many minutes does it take?

B. 15(십오)분쯤 걸려요.   It takes about 15 minutes.

☞ 문법   Grammar

1. '-었어요.'

   (1) '-었어요.' is a past tense ending.

   (2) '-었어요.' follows vowels such as '어' '여' '우' '유' '으' '이'
      ('Yin' or dark vowels).

감기 걸렸어요?	Have you caught a cold?
감기 걸렸어요.	I've caught a cold.
10분 걸렸어요?	Did it take 10 minutes?
10분 걸렸어요.	It took 10 minutes.

2. -았어요.

   (1) The meaning of '-았어요' is the same as '-었어요.'

   (2) '-았어요' follows syllables with vowels such as '아' '야' '오'
      '요'('Yang' or bright vowels).

병원에 갔어요?	Did you go to a hospital?
병원에 갔어요.	I went to a hospital.
안 갔어요?	Didn't you go?
안 갔어요.	I didn't go.

   ＊The past tense of 해요 is 했어요.

3. -이

   (1) There is no big difference between '발 아파요.' and '발이 아파요.'

   (2) The subject marker, '-이'(or '-가') is optional in conversation.

아파요.	(It) hurts.
발 아파요.	(My) feet hurt.
발이 아파요.	(My) feet hurt.
아직 발이 아파요.	(My) feet still hurt.

4. 걸리다   catch (a cold), to take (time)

걸리세요?	걸려요.
걸리셨어요?	걸렸어요.

5. 아프다   hurt

아프세요?   아파요.
아프셨어요?   아팠어요.

▨ 연습   Practice

1. Change to past tense.
   (1) 자주 아파요?
   (2) 가끔 아파요.
   (3) 안 가요?
   (4) 안 가요.
   (5) 한국어 공부해요.

2. Translate into Korean.
   (1) Where does it hurt?
   (2) I have a headache.
   (3) I don't know.
   (4) I've caught a cold.
   (5) Did you go to a hospital?

제 14 과   어서 오세요.

Lesson 14   Come on in!

❋어휘   Vocabulary

어서	to ahead and	기다리다	to wait
방	room	온돌	(Korean heating system)
예약	reservation	지난	last, past
예약하다	to make a reservation	주	week
며칠	how many days	성함	name(honorific)
계시다	to stay(honorific)	어떻게	how
하루	one day	-호실	room no
잠깐	a moment	밝다	to be bright
-만	only, just		

* '온돌' is the traditional Korean heating system. The floor is heated from the below, warming the whole room.

A. 어서 오세요.　　　　　Come on in, please.

B. 방 있어요?　　　　　　Do you have a room?

A. 예약하셨어요?　　　　Did you make a reservation?

B. 아니오.　　　　　　　No.

A. 며칠동안 계시겠어요?　How many days do you want to
　　　　　　　　　　　　stay?

B. 하루요.　　　　　　　One day.

A. 잠깐만 기다리세요.　　Wait a moment, please.

B. 아, 온돌 방을 주세요.　Ah, I want a Korean-style room.

* * * * * * * * *

A. 지난 주에 예약을 했어요.　I made a reservation last
　　　　　　　　　　　　　week.

B. 성함이 어떻게 되세요?　What's your name?

A. 스미스인데요.　　　　My name is Smith.

B. 잠깐만 기다리세요.　　Wait a minute, please.

　　아, 네, 여기 있어요.　Oh, yes, your name is here.

　　210(이백십)호실입니다.　It is Room 210.

A. 밝은 방이에요?　　　　Is it a sunny room?

B. 네, 좋은 방이에요.　　Yes, it's a nice room.

1. '쓰' in front of 'ㄷ' is pronounced as [ㄷ] : 했다 [핻다] → [해따]
2. In front of 'ㄴ', '쓰' is pronounced as [ㄴ] : 했는데요[핸는데요]
3. The pronunciation of '밝다' is [박따].
4. In front of vowels, the 'ㄹ' in '리' is not silent : 밝은[발근]

☞ 문법   Grammar

1. -셨어요?
   (1) '-셨어요?' is an honorific past tense ending.
   (2) '-셨어요?' is used when the preceding syllable ends with a vowel.

   예약하|셨어요?   Did you make a reservation?
   기다리|셨어요?   Did you wait?
   주|셨어요?   Did you give (it)?

2. -시겠어요?
   (1) '-시겠어요?' means 'Will you - ?'.
   (2) '-시겠어요?' follows verb roots which end with a vowel.

   오|시겠어요?   Will you come?
   가|시겠어요?   Will you go?
   사|시겠어요?   Will you buy (it)?

3. -만   only

   기다리세요.   Please wait.
   잠깐만 기다리세요.   Please wait a moment.
   여기서 잠깐만 기다리세요.   Please wait here a moment.

4. 기다리다   wait

   기다리세요?   기다려요.
   기다리셨어요?   기다렸어요.

5. 주다   give

주세요?	줘요.
주셨어요?	줬어요.

▨ 연습 Practice

1. Fill in the blanks.

   (1) Will you make a reservation?   예약하 |_____

      Will you wait?   기다리 |_____

      Will you give (me)?   주 |_____

   (2) Did you come?   오 |_____

      Did you go?   가 |_____

      Did you buy (it)?   사 |_____

2. Translate into Korean.

   (1) Come on in, please.

   (2) Did you make a reservation?

   (3) How many days will you stay?

   (4) Wait a moment, please.

   (5) What's your name?

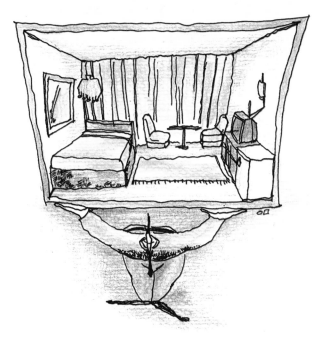

제 15 과 　 한국에 언제 오셨어요?

Lesson 15 　 When did you come to Korea?

❀ 어휘 　 Vocabulary

한국	Korea	얼마나	how long
언제	when	걸리다	to take (time)
작년	last year	한	one
삼	3	시간	hour
월	month	뭐	what
살다	to live	일	work
학교	school	무슨	what kind
멀다	to be far	은행	bank

A. 한국에 언제 오셨어요?　　When did you come to Korea?

B. 작년 삼월에 왔어요.　　I came here last March.

A. 어디에서 사세요?　　Where do you live?

B. 신촌에 살아요.　　I live in Shin-ch'on.

A. 학교에서 멀어요?　　Is it far from the school?

B. 네, 좀 멀어요.　　Yes, it is a little far.

A. 얼마나 걸려요?　　How long does it take?

B. 한 시간쯤 걸려요.　　It takes about 1 hour.

* * * * * * * * *

A. 한국에서 뭐 하세요?　　What do you do in Korea?

B. 일해요.　　I work.

A. 무슨 일 하세요?　　What kind of work do you do?

B. 은행에 다녀요.　　I work in a bank.

A. 무슨 은행이오?　　Which bank?

B. 한국 은행이오.　　The Bank of Korea.

A. 어디 있어요?　　Where is it?

B. 명동에 있어요.　　It is in Myŏng-dong.

☎ 발음   Pronunciation

1. In front of ' ㄴ ', ' ㄱ ' is pronounced as [ㅇ] : 작년[장년]
2. The sound of 멀 in 멀다 is a little longer than other syllables.
3. The pronunciation of ' ㄹ ' in 멀다 is similar to [l], but the tip of the tongue should touch the roof of the mouth, rather than the front teeth.
4. In front of vowels, however, the sound of ' ㄹ ' is close to an Italian or Spanish [r] : 멀어요[머러요]

☞ 문법   Grammar

1. -어요. (cf. p. 52)

| 학교에서 멀 | 어요? | Is (it) far from the school? |
| 학교에서 멀 | 어요. | (It) is far from the school. |

| 어디 있 | 어요? | Where is (it)? |
| 집에 있 | 어요. | (It) is at home. |

2. -해요. (cf. p. 56)

(1) The basic form of ' -해요 ' is ' -하다 '(c.f. p.56).

(2) The words in front of ' -해요 ' are usually independent nouns. For example, ' 숙제 ' is a noun meaning 'homework', and ' 숙제 해요 ' is a verb meaning 'I'm doing homework.'

| 숙제 | 해요? | Are (you) doing (your) homework? |
| 숙제 | 해요. | (I) am doing (my) homework. |

| 공부 | 해요? | Are (you) working? |
| 공부 | 해요. | (I) am working. |

3. -에서   in (a place)

해요.	(I) do (something).
일해요.	(I) work.
한국에서 일해요.	(I) work in Korea.

4. 오다   come

'오+아오' is contracted into '와요.'

오세요?   와요
오셨어요.   왔어요.

5. 살다   live

The final consonant 'ㄹ' of '살' –is dropped before 'ㅅ'of '–세요.'

사세요?   살아요.
사셨어요?   살았어요.

▨ 연습   Practice

1. Fill in the blanks.
   (1) When did you go to France?   프랑스(   ) 언제 가셨어요?
   (2) I came here in January.   일월(   ) 왔어요.
   (3) Where do you study?   어디(   ) 공부하세요?
   (4) Is it near the post office? 우체국(   ) 가까워요?
   (5) What did you do in China?   중국(   ) 뭐 하셨어요?

2. Translate into Korean.
   (1) It is far.
   (2) How long does it take?
   (3) It takes 20 minutes.
   (4) What kind of work do you do?
   (5) Where is it?

Sino-Korean numbers		Classifiers	Modifiers		Classifiers	
1	일	월 (January)	1	한	달	month
10	십	분 minutes	2	두	시	o'clock
100	백	층 floors	10	열	시간	hours
1000	천	년 years	20	스무	개	pieces
10000	만	원 wŏn	100	백	장	sheets

제 16 과   이 수박 얼마예요?

Lesson 16   How much is this watermelon?

❀ 어휘   Vocabulary

수박	watermelon	돈	money
천	1,000	내다	to pay
너무	too	냈어요.	I paid.
사과	apple	잔돈	small change
두	two	받다	to receive
개	(counting unit)	받았어요.	I received (it).

☎ 발음   Pronunciation

1. 받다 [바따]   2. 받았어요 [바다써요]

A. 이 수박 얼마예요?　　　How much is this watermelon?

B. 만 오천원이에요.　　　It is 15,000 won.

A. 너무 비싸요.　　　It is too expensive.

　　좀 싼 것 없어요?　　　Don't you have a little cheaper one?

B. 이것은 만원이에요.　　　This one is 10,000 won.

A. 이 사과는 얼마예요?　　　How much are these apples?

B. 천원이에요.　　　They are 1,000 won.

A. 두 개 주세요.　　　Please give me two.

B. 여기 있어요.　　　Here you are.

* * * * * * * * *

A. 돈 냈어요?　　　Did you pay?

B. 냈어요.　　　Yes.

A. 얼마 냈어요?　　　How much did you pay?

B. 이 만원 냈어요.　　　I paid 20,000 won.

A. 잔돈 받았어요?　　　Did you receive the change?

B. 네, 받았어요.　　　Yes, I did.

A. 얼마 받았어요?　　　How much did you receive?

B. 팔천원 받았어요.　　　8,000 won.

☞ 문법   Grammar

1. -ㅆ어요.

　(1) '-ㅆ어요' is a past tense ending.

　(2) '-ㅆ어요' follows verb roots ending with a vowel.

돈 냈어요?	Did you pay?
돈 냈어요.	I paid.
학교에 갔어요?	Did you go to school?
학교에 갔어요.	I went to school.

2. -았어요. (cf. p. 60)

　(1) '-았어요' is a past tense ending

　(2) '-았어요' follows verb roots ending with a consonant.

돈 받았어요?	Did you receive the money?
돈 받았어요.	I received the money.
숙제가 많았어요?	Did you have a lot of homework?
숙제가 많았어요.	I had a lot of homework.

3. -개

　(1) '-개' is a counting unit

　(2) Pure Korean cardinal numbers are used in front of '- 개.'

주세요.	Give me.
사과 주세요.	Give me (an) apple.
이 사과 주세요.	Give me this apple.
이 사과 두 개 주세요.	Give me two of these apples.

4. 내다   pay

내세요?	내요.
내셨어요?	냈어요.

5. 받다   receive

받으세요?	받아요.

-72-

받으셨어요?   받았어요.

▨ 연습   Practice

1. Fill in the blank.

    (1) Give me| three of these apples.   이 사과   ____| 개 주세요.

          Give me| four of those watermelons. 저 수박   ____| 개 주세요.

          Give me| five of these oranges.   이 오렌지   ____| 개 주세요.

    (2) It is 2,000 won.   ____| 원이에요.

          It is 30,000 won.   ____| 원이에요.

          It is 45,000 won.   ____| 원이에요.

2. Translate into Korean.

    (1) It is too expensive.

    (2) Don't you have a little cheaper one?

    (3) I paid 1,000 won.

    (4) I received the change.

    (5) I haven't received the change.

제 17 과   바빠요?

Lesson 17   Are you busy?

바쁘다	to be busy	시간	time
많다	to be a lot	언제나	always
무슨	what kind of	가끔	sometimes
회사	company, firm	내일	tommorrow

☎ 발음 Pronunciation

1. 많다 [만타]   2. 많이 [마니]

A. 바빠요?　　　　　　 Are you busy?

B. 네, 바빠요.　　　　　 Yes, I'm busy.

A. 왜 바빠요?　　　　　 Why are you busy?

B. 일이 많아요.　　　　 I have a lot of work.

A. 무슨 일이오?　　　　 What kind of work?

B. 회사 일이오.　　　　 Office work.

A. 언제나 바빠요?　　　 Are you always busy?

B. 네, 언제나 바빠요.　 Yes, I'm always busy.

* * * * * * * * *

A. 시간 있어요?　　　　 Do you have free time?

B. 없어요.　　　　　　　 No.

A. 왜요?　　　　　　　　 Why?

B. 바빠요.　　　　　　　 I'm busy.

A. 언제나 바빠요?　　　 Are you always busy?

B. 아니오, 가끔 바빠요.　No. I'm only busy sometimes.

A. 내일은 시간 있어요?　Do you have free time tomorrow?

B. 내일은 시간 있어요.　I have free time tomorrow.

☞ 문법 Grammar

1. -어요.(cf. p. 48, 52, 68)

시간 있l어요?	Do you have free time?
시간 있l어요.	I have free time.
돈 없l어요?	Don't you have money?
돈 없l어요.	I don't have money.

2. -아요(cf. p. 52)

(1) '-아요' is a basic verb ending.

(2) '-아요' follows syllables containing the 'Yang' vowels.

(3) The basic form of 바빠요 is 바쁘다. This has a 'Yin' vowel, and is an exeption. '으' is a very weak vowel, and is often omitted in this way.

바빠요?	Are you busy?
바빠요.	I am busy.

3. -은(cf. p. 48)

(1) '-은' is a topic marker.

(2) '-은' follows syllables that end with a consonant.

있어요.	I have (it).
시간 있어요.	I have free time.
내일 시간 있어요.	I have free time tomorrow.
*내일은 시간 있어요.	I have free time tomorrow.

*The '-은' limits what you are saying('시간 있어요.') to 'tomorrow', and implies that on the other days you might not have free time.

4. 바쁘다 be busy

바쁘세요?	바빠요.
바쁘셨어요?	바빴어요.

5. 있다 have

있으세요?   있어요.

있으셨어요?   있었어요.

⊞ 연습   Practice

1. Change to '-아요/-어요' form.

   (1) 바쁘다

   (2) 많다

   (3) 있다

   (4) 없다

   (5) 가다

2. Translate into Korean.

   (1) Are you always busy?

   (2) Do you have free time?

   (3) Do you have a lot of work?

   (4) I have a lot of books.

   (5) I have a lot of time.

제 18 과　　표 한 장에 얼마예요?

Lesson 18　　How much is it for one ticket?

❋ 어휘　Vocabulary

표	ticket	주	week
장	(counting unit for tickets)	영화	movie
–에	for	보다	to see
얼마	how much	지난	last
학생	student	재미있다	to be interesting
입구	entrance		

☎ 발음　Pronunciation

1. 재미있다 [재미읻다] → [재미이따]
2. 재미있어요 [재미이써요]

A. 표 한 장에 얼마예요?   How much is it for one ticket?
B. 오천원이에요.   It is 5,000 won.

A. 학생은 얼마예요?   How much is it for students?
B. 학생은 사천원이에요.   For students it is 4,000 won.

A. 학생표 두 장 주세요.   Give me two student tickets.
B. 여기 있어요.   Here you are.

A. 입구가 어디예요?   Where is the entrance?
B. 저쪽이에요.   Over there.

* * * * * * * *

A. 이 영화 보셨어요?   Have you seen this movie?
C. 네, 봤어요.   Yes, I have.

A. 언제 보셨어요?   When did you see it?
C. 지난 주에 봤어요.   I saw it last week.

A. 재미있으셨어요?   Did you enjoy it?
C. 네, 재미있었어요.   Yes, I enjoyed it.

A. 어느 나라 영화예요?   What country is that movie from?
C. 프랑스 영화예요.   It is a French movie.

☞ 문법   Grammar

1. -셨어요? (cf. p. 64)

   (1) '-셨어요' is an honorific past tense ending
   (2) '-셨어요' follows verb roots which end with a vowel.

   주|셨어요?   Did you give (it)?
   보|셨어요?   Did you see (it)?
   사|셨어요?   Did you buy (it)?

2. -으셨어요?

   (1) '-으셨어요' is an honorific past tense ending
   (2) '-으셨어요' follows verb roots which end with a consonant.

   재미있|으셨어요?   Did you enjoy (it)?
   돈 받|으셨어요?   Did you receive the money?
   전화 받|으셨어요?   Did you get the phone?

3. -를

   (1) -를 is an object marker
   (2) -를 follows nouns which end with a vowel.
   (3) The object markers are optional in conversation.

   봤어요.   I saw (it).
   영화 봤어요.   I saw a movie.
   영화를 봤어요.   I saw a movie.
   좋은 영화를 봤어요. I saw a good movie.

4. 보다   see

   보세요?   봐요.
   보셨어요?   봤어요.

5. 재미있다   have fun

   재미있으세요?   재미있어요.
   재미있으셨어요?   재미있었어요.

1. Fill in the blanks.

   (1) Did you| study?   공부하 |------------

        Did you| pay (it)?   돈 내 |------------

        Did you| write (it)?   쓰 |------------

   (2) Did you| read (it)?   읽 |------------

        Did you| receive the change? 잔돈 받 |------------

        Did| you sit down?   앉 |------------

2. Translate into Korean.

   (1) How much is it for one ticket?

   (2) Give me three tickets.

   (3) Where is the entrance?

   (4) Over there.

   (5) It is 5,000 won.

제 19 과　여보세요?

Lesson 19　Hello?

❀ 어휘　Vocabulary

여보세요?	Hello?	들어오다	to come in
말씀하다	to speak(honorific)	오후	afternoon
선생님	teacher, you(hon.)	여섯	six
저	I(humble)	그러면	then
댁	residence	다시	again
-인가요?	(a verb ending)	전화하다	to make a phone call
맞다	to be correct	-겠습니다	I will -
-는데요	(a verb ending)		

☏ 발음　Pronunciation

1. 맞다 [맏다] → [마따]
2. 맞는데요 [만는데요]

A. 여보세요.   Hello?

B. 말씀하세요.   I'm listening.

A. 김선생님 계세요?   Is Mr. Kim there?

B. 전데요.   This is he.

A. 아, 안녕하세요.   Oh, how are you?

   저예요.   It's me.

B. 아, 박선생님이세요?   Oh, are you Mrs. Park?

   안녕하셨어요?   How have you been?

* * * * * * * * *

A. 여보세요.   Hello?

B. 거기 박선생님 댁인가요? Is this Mrs. Park's residence?

A. 네, 맞는데요.   That's right.

B. 선생님 계세요?   Is she home?

A. 지금 안 계신데요.   She is not in now.

B. 언제쯤 들어오세요?   When will she be in?

A. 오후 여섯 시쯤 들어오세요. She will be in about 6 p.m.

B. 네, 그러면 다시 전화하겠습니다. I see. I'll call back, then.

☞ 문법   Grammar

1. -ㄴ데요.

   (1) '-ㄴ데요' suggests that the preceding information carries some extra significance, beyond what is stated literally.

   (2) '-ㄴ데요' follows -이다(to be) and descriptive verbs.

전데요.	This is he/she.
집인데요.	This is his house(family member).
안 계신데요.	He's not here right now.

2. -는데요.

   (1) '-는데요' has the same meaning as '-ㄴ데요.'

   (2) '-는데요' follows all verb roots except '-이다.'

맞는데요.	That's right.
주무시는데요.	He's asleep.
들어오시는데요.	He's coming in.

3. -에   at (time)

전화하겠습니다.	I will call.
다시 전화하겠습니다.	I will call back.
여섯 시에 다시 전화하겠습니다.	I will call back at 6:00.

4. 들어오다   come in

들어오세요?	들어와요.
들어오셨어요?	들어왔어요.

5. 전화하다   call

전화하세요?	전화해요.
전화하셨어요?	전화했어요.

1. Change to '-ㄴ데요/-는데요' form.

    (1) 오다

    (2) 가다

    (3) 보다

    (4) 읽다

    (5) 재미있다

2. Translate into Korean.

    (1) Hello?

    (2) Is Mr. /Mrs. Han there?

    (3) This is he/she.

    (4) She is not in now.

    (5) I will call back.

제 20 과   점심 먹었어요?

Lesson 20   Did you have lunch?

❀ 어휘   Vocabulary

점심	lunch	배고프다	to be hungry
시	o'clock	-지 않다	not to -
매일	every day	식사하다	to eat
보통	usually	들다	to eat(honorific)
식당	restaurant, cafeteria	냉면	cold noodles

☏ 발음   Pronunciation

1. 몇 시 [멷시] → [며씨]   2. 먹었어요 [머거써요]

A. 점심 먹었어요?   Did you have lunch?

B. 네, 먹었어요.   Yes I did.

A. 언제 먹었어요?   When did you eat?

B. 한 시에 먹었어요.   I ate at 1 o'clock.

A. 매일 한 시에 먹어요?   Do you eat at 1 o'clock every day?

B. 보통 한 시에 먹어요.   I usually eat at 1 o'clock.

A. 어디에서 먹어요?   Where do you eat?

B. 식당에서 먹어요.   I eat in the restaurant.

* * * * * * * *

A. 배고프세요?   Are you hungry?

B. 아니오, 배고프지 않아요.   No, I'm not hungry.

A. 몇 시에 식사하셨어요?   What time did you eat?

B. 한 시에 먹었어요.   I ate at 1 o'clock.

A. 뭐 드셨어요?   What did you eat?

B. 냉면 먹었어요.   I ate Naeng-myn?

A. 맛있었어요?   Was it good?

B. 맛있었어요.   It was good.

☞ 문법   Grammar

1. -지 않아요.

   (1) '-지 않아요' is a negative ending

   (2) '-지 않아요' follows verb roots.

배고프	지 않아요?	Aren't you	hungry?
배고프	지 않아요.	I am not	hungry.
맛있	지 않아요?	Isn't it	good?
맛있	지 않아요.	It isn't	good.

2. -지 않으세요.

   (1) '-지 않으세요' is an honorific negative ending.

   (2) '-지 않으세요' follows verb roots.

식당에서 드시지 않으세요?	Don't you eat in the cafeteria?
식당에서 먹지 않아요.	I don't eat in the cafeteria.
맛있지 않으세요?	Isn't it good?
맛있지 않아요.	It isn't good.

3. -을

   (1) '-을' is an object marker

   (2) '-을' follows nouns which end with a consonant.

먹었어요.	I ate.
비빔밥 먹었어요.	I ate Pibim-bap.
비빔밥을 먹었어요.	I ate Pibim-bap.
오늘 비빔밥을 먹었어요.	I ate Pibim-bap today.

4. 배고프다   be hungry

   | 배고프세요? | 배고파요. |
   | 배고프셨어요? | 배고팠어요. |

5. 배고프지 않다   be not hungry

   | 배고프지 않으세요? | 배고프지 않아요. |
   | 배고프지 않으셨어요? | 배고프지 않았어요. |

1. Change to past tense.
   (1) 아침 먹어요.
   (2) 먹지 않아요.
   (3) 배고파요.
   (4) 배고프지 않아요.
   (5) 맛있어요.

2. Translate into Korean.
   (1) Where do you have lunch?
   (2) What time do you go to school?
   (3) Do you eat in the cafeteria?
   (4) I am very hungry.
   (5) I am not hungry yet.

제 21 과   어떤 것을 찾으세요?

Lesson 21   What kind of thing are you looking for?

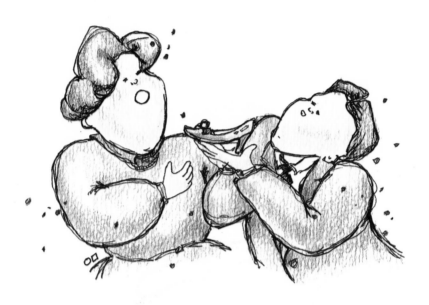

❀ 어휘   Vocabulary

어떤	what kind of	신어보다	to try(shoes) on
찾다	to look for, to find	-ㄹ까요?	Shall I -
흰색	white	어떠세요	How do you like-
구두	(dress) shoes	좀	a little
이쪽	this way	크다	to be big
-으로	to	그렇지만	however
마음에 들다	to be appealing	낮다	to be low, short
높다	to be high, tall	그러면	then, in that case

☎ 발음   Pronunciation

1. 찾다 [찬다] → [차따]   2. 찾으세요 [차즈세요]

3. 낮다 [낟다] → [나따]   4. 낮아요 [나자요]

-90-

A. 어떤 것을 찾으세요?　　　What kind of thing are you
　　　　　　　　　　　　　looking for?

B. 흰색 구두 있어요?　　　　Do you have white shoes?

A. 네, 이쪽으로 오세요.　　　Yes, come this way.

B. 이거 괜찮은데요.　　　　These are not bad.

A. 마음에 드세요?　　　　　Do you like them?

B. 네, 마음에 들어요.　　　Yes, I like them.

B. 신어볼까요?　　　　　　Shall I try them on?

A. 네, 신어보세요.　　　　Yes, try them on.

* * * * * * * * *

A. 이것은 어떠세요?　　　How about these?

B. 좀 커요.　　　　　　　They are a little big.

A. 이것도 커요?　　　　　Are these also big?

B. 아니오. 그렇지만 너무　　No. They're too low, though.
　　낮아요.

A. 그러면 이것은 어떠세요?　How about these, then?

B. 너무 높아요.　　　　　They're too high.

A. 이것은 마음에 드세요?　Do you like these, (then)?

B. 네, 좋아요.　　　　　Yes, they're nice.

☞ 문법   Grammar

1. -ㄹ까요?

   (1) '-ㄹ까요' means "Shall I -".

   (2) '-ㄹ까요' follows verb roots ending with a vowel.

신어볼까요?	Shall I| try them on?
갈까요?	Shall I| go?
일할까요?	Shall I| work?

2. -을까요?

   (1) '-을까요' means "Shall I -".

   (2) '-을까요' follows verb roots ending with a consonant.

찾|을까요?	Shall I| look (it) for?
신|을까요?	Shall I| wear (the shoes)?
입|을까요?	Shall I| wear (the clothes)?

3. -으로

   (1) '-으로' means to (a place)

   (2) '-으로' follows nouns ending with a consonant.

오세요.	Come (here)
이쪽으로 오세요.	Come this way.
빨리 이쪽으로 오세요.	Come this way quickly.

4. 찾다   look for

찾으세요?	찾아요.
찾으셨어요.	찾았어요.

5. 마음에 들다   like

마음에 드세요?	마음에 들어요.
마음에 드셨어요?	마음에 들었어요.

▨ 연습 Practice

1. Change to -ㄹ까요/-을까요 form.
   (1) 공부하다
   (2) 먹다
   (3) 오다
   (4) 보다
   (5) 전화하다

2. Translate into Korean.
   (1) Go that way.
   (2) Do you like it?
   (3) I like it.
   (4) What do you think about this book?
   (5) Do you have any money?

제 22 과   어떤 것을 넣으시겠어요?

Lesson 22   Which one do you want to put in?

❀ 어휘   Vocabulary

어떤	which	-을까요?	Shall I -
-을	(object marker)	가득	full
넣다	to put in	-어 드릴까요?	Do you want me to
보통	normal	어치	worth of
휘발유	gasoline	카드	(credit)card
-를	(object marker)	사인하다	to sign
-어 주세요	Please do -	수고하다	to work hard

☎ 발음   Pronunciation

1. 넣다 [너타]   2. 넣을까요[너을까요]

A. 어떤 것을 넣으시겠어요?   Which one do you want
                              to put in?
B. 보통휘발유를 넣어 주세요.   Regular gasoline, please.

A. 얼마나 넣을까요?   How much do you want me
                              to put in?
B. 가득 넣어 주세요.   Fill it up, please.

A. 얼마예요?   How much is it?
B. 만 오천원인데요.   It is 15,000 won.

A. 여기 있어요.   Here you are.
B. 안녕히 가세요.   Good-bye!

* * * * * * * * *

A. 얼마나 넣어 드릴까요?   How much do you want me
                              to put in?
B. 만원어치 넣어 주세요.   Please put in 10,000 won worth.

A. 다 됐습니다.   All done.
B. 카드로 내겠어요.   I'll pay by credit card.

A. 사인해 주세요.   Sign, please.
B. 여기 있어요.   Here you are.

A. 안녕히 가세요.   Good-bye!
B. 수고하셨어요.   Thanks.

☞ 문법 Grammar

1. -으시겠어요?(cf. p. 64)

  (1) '-으시겠어요?' means "Would you like to -?".

  (2) '-으시겠어요?' follows verb roots which end with a consonant.

얼마나 넣|으시겠어요? How much |would you like to put in?

뭐 넣|으시겠어요?   What |would you like to put in?

가득 넣|으시겠어요? |Would you like to fill it up?

2. -어 드릴까요?

  (1) '-어 드릴까요?' means "Do you want me to -".

  (2) '-어 드릴까요?' follows verb roots which end with a consonant.

보통휘발유 넣|어 드릴까요? Do you want me to| put in normal gas?

가득 넣|어 드릴까요? Do you want me to| fill it up?

만원어치 넣|어 드릴까요? Do you want me to| put in 10,000 won worth?

3. -어 주세요.

  (1) '-어 주세요' means "Please do -".

  (2) '-어 주세요' follows verb roots which end with a consonant.

넣어 주세요. Please put in.

가득 넣어 주세요. Please fill it up.

보통휘발유 가득 넣어 주세요. Please fill it up with normal gas.

4. 넣다 put in

넣으세요?   넣어요.

넣으셨어요?   넣었어요.

5. 가다 go

가세요?   가요.

가셨어요?   갔어요.

1. Fill in the blanks.

    (1)   Do you want to |read (it)?   읽 |_____

    (2) Do you want me to |read (it)?   읽 |_____

    (3)   Please |read (it).   읽 |_____

    (4)   Did you |read (it)?   읽 |_____

    (5)   Don't you |read (it)?   읽 |_____

2. Translate into Korean.

    (1) Give me 4,000 won worth.

    (2) I'll pay by credit card.

    (3) Do you want to wear (the shoes)?

    (4) Fill it up, please.

    (5) All done.

제 23 과   이 옷 세탁해 주세요.

Lesson 23   Wash this piece of clothing, please.

✽ 어휘   Vocabulary

이	this, these	내다	to pay
옷	clothes	찾다	to get (it) back
세탁하다	to wash (clothes)	-을 때	when to -
드라이 클리닝	dry cleaning	알다	to know
며칠	how many days	맡기다	to entrust
걸리다	to take (time)	그저께	the day before yesterday
모레	the day after tomorrow	코트	coat
돈	money	이거	this one
지금	now	맞다	to be correct

☎ 발음   Pronunciation

1. 맞다 [맏다] → [마따]   2. 맞아요 [마자요]

-98-

A. 이 옷 세탁해 주세요.   Wash this piece of clothing, please.
B. 드라이 클리닝이에요?   Dry cleaning?

A. 네. 며칠 걸려요?   Yes. How many days will it take?
B. 모레 오세요.   Come back the day after tomorrow.

A. 돈은 지금 내요?   Should I pay now?
B. 아니오. 옷 찾을 때에 내세요.   No. Pay when you pick it up.

A. 알겠습니다. 안녕히 계세요.   I see. Bye!
B. 안녕히 가세요.   Bye!

* * * * * * * *

A. 옷 찾으러 왔어요.   I'm here to pick up my piece of clothing.
B. 언제 맡기셨어요?   When did you leave it here?

A. 그저께 맡겼는데요.   I left it here the day before yesterday.
B. 뭐 맡기셨어요?   What did you leave here?

A. 코트예요.   It's a coat.
B. 이거예요?   Is this it?

A. 네, 맞아요.   Yes, right.
B. 오천원이에요.   5000 won, please.

☞ 문법 Grammar

1. -해 주세요.   Please do -

        세탁|해 주세요.   Please| wash this.

   드라이클리닝|해 주세요.   Please| dry clean this.

      전화|해 주세요.   Please| call me.

2. -으러

  (1) '-으러' means "in order to -".

  (2) '-으러' follows verb roots which end with a consonant.

옷 찾|으러 왔어요?   Did you come |to pick up your clothes?

옷 찾|으러 왔어요.   I came |to pick up my clothes.

밥 먹|으러 갔어요?   Did he go |to eat?

밥 먹|으러 갔어요.   He went |to eat.

3. - 지 마세요.   Please don't do -

       내세요.   Please pay.

      돈 내세요.   Please pay the money.

   지금 돈 내세요.   Please pay the money now.

 지금 돈 내지 마세요.   Please don't pay the money now.

4. 알다   know

   아세요?   알아요.

   아셨어요?   알았어요.

5. 맡기다   entrust

   맡기세요?   맡겨요.

   맡기셨어요?   맡겼어요.

▨ 연습 Practice

1. Change to '-세요' form.
   (1) 가다
   (2) 오다
   (3) 찾다
   (4) 세탁하다
   (5) 맡기다

2. Translate into Korean.
   (1) Wash this piece of clothing, please.
   (2) How many days will it take?
   (3) Come back tomorrow.
   (4) I see.
   (5) It is 7,500 won.

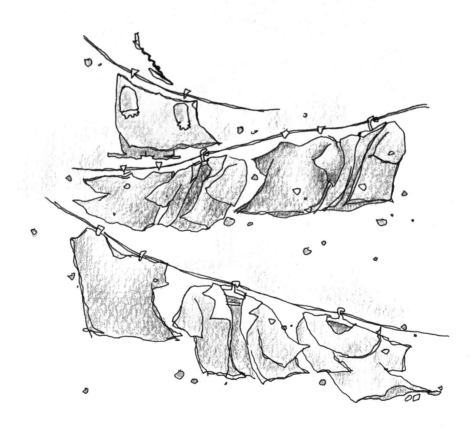

제 24 과   그 사람 만났어요?

Lesson 24   Did you meet that person?

❀ 어휘   Vocabulary

그	that	알다	to know
사람	person	어떻게	how
만나다	to meet	친구	friend
어디서	where	-의	of ('s)
다방	tea house	학생	student
사월	April	-에서	at (a place)
자주	often	가끔	occasionally

☎ 발음   Pronunciation

1. 작년 [장년]   2. 알았어요 [아라써요]

A. 그 사람 만났어요?   Did you meet that person?

B. 네, 만났어요.   Yes, I did.

A. 어디서 만났어요?   Where did you meet him?

B. 다방에서 만났어요.   I met him in a tea house.

A. 언제 만났어요?   When did you meet him?

B. 사월 일일에 만났어요.   I met him on April 1st.

A. 자주 만나요?   Do you see him often?

B. 가끔 만나요.   I see him from time to time.

* * * * * * * *

A. 그 사람 언제 알았어요?   When did you come to know him?

B. 작년에 알았어요.   I came to know him last year.

A. 어떻게 알았어요?   How did you come to know him?

B. 친구의 친구예요.   He is a friend of a friend.

A. 학생이에요?   Is he a student?

B. 네, 학생이에요.   Yes, he is a student.

A 학교에서 만났어요?   Did you meet him at school?

B. 네, 학교에서 만났어요.   Yes, I met him at school.

☞ 문법   Grammar

1. -ㅆ어요(cf. p.72)

   (1) '-ㅆ어요' is a past tense ending

   (2) '-ㅆ어요' follows verb roots ending with a vowel.

친구 만났어요?	Did you meet your friend?
친구 만났어요.	I met my friend.
그 사람 갔어요?	Did he/she leave?
그 사람 갔어요.	He/she left.

2. -았어요.(cf. p. 60, 70)

   (1) '-았어요' is a past tense ending

   (2) '-았어요' follows verb roots ending with a consonant.

언제 알았어요?	When did you come to know (him)?
작년에 알았어요.	I came to know (him) last year.
옷 찾았어요?	Did you pick up your clothes?
옷 찾았어요.	I picked up my clothes.

3. -에서 at(a place)(cf. p. 68)

만나요.	I meet (her).
자주 만나요.	I meet (her) often.
학교에서 자주 만나요.	I meet (her) often at school.
그 사람 학교에서 자주 만나요.	I meet her often at school.

4. 만나다   meet

만나세요?	만나요.
만나셨어요?	만났어요.

1. Change to past tense.
   (1) 매일 학교에 가요.
   (2) 그 선생님 만나요.
   (3) 식당에서 먹어요.
   (4) 도서관에서 공부해요.
   (5) 책 읽어요.

2. Translate into Korean.
   (1) When did you meet him?
   (2) Where did you study?
   (3) What did you read?
   (4) Where did you go?
   (5) What did you eat?

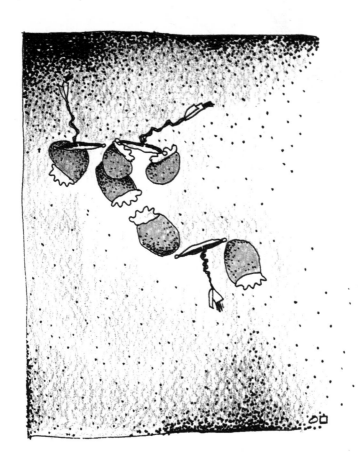

제 25 과　　언제 왔어요?

Lesson 25　　When did you come here?

❀ 어휘　Vocabulary

어제	yesterday	그	that
친구	friend	가다	to go
안	not	토요일	Saturday
바쁘다	to be busy	-에	at(time)
-아서	because	집	house
못	cannot	부산	Pusan(city name)

☎ 발음　Pronunciation

1. 못 왔어요 [몯 와써요] → [모돠써요]
2. 집에　　[지베]

A. 언제 왔어요?　　　When did you come here?

B. 어제 왔어요.　　　I came here yesterday.

A. 친구도 왔어요?　　Did your friend come, too?

B. 친구는 안 왔어요.　He didn't come.

A. 왜 안 왔어요?　　　Why not?

B. 바빠서 못 왔어요.　He couldn't come because he was busy.

A. 바빠요?　　　　　He is busy?

B. 네, 바빠요.　　　　Yes, he is busy.

* * * * * * * *

A. 그 친구 갔어요?　　Did your friend leave?

B. 네, 갔어요.　　　　Yes, he did.

A. 언제 갔어요?　　　When did he leave?

B. 토요일에 갔어요.　He went on Saturday.

A. 어디 갔어요?　　　Where did he go?

B. 집에 갔어요.　　　He went home.

A. 집이 어디예요?　　Where is his home?

B. 부산이에요.　　　Pusan.

☞ 문법   Grammar

1. -았어요(cf. p.60, 72,104)

   (1) '-았어요' is a past tense ending

   (2) '-았어요' follows verb roots ending with '오.'

안 왔어요?	Didn't he come?
안 왔어요.	He didn't come.
신문 봤어요?	Didn't you read/see the newspaper?
신문 봤어요.	I read/saw the newspaper.

2. -ㅆ어요.(cf. p. 72, 104)

   (1) -ㅆ어요 is a past tense ending.

   (2) -ㅆ어요 follows verb roots ending with a vowel.

그 친구 갔어요?	Did that friend leave?
그 친구 갔어요.	That friend left.
옷 샀어요?	Did you buy some clothes?
옷 샀어요.	I bought some clothes.

3. -에   to (a place)

                 갔어요. (He) went.

           집에 갔어요. (He) went home.

    수요일에 집에 갔어요. (He) went home on Wednesday.

그 친구 수요일에 집에 갔어요. That friend went home on Wednesday.

4. 요일   days of the week

월요일	Monday
화요일	Tuesday
수요일	Wednesday
목요일	Thursday
금요일	Friday
토요일	Saturday
일요일	Sunday

圖 연습   Practice

1. Change to past tense.
   (1) 매일 바빠요.
   (2) 신문 봐요.
   (3) 옷 사요.
   (4) 극장에 가요.
   (5) 집에 와요.

2. Translate into Korean.
   (1) When did you come home?
   (2) Who bought these clothes?
   (3) When will you go home?
   (4) What time is it?
   (5) What is it?

Appendices

* The Korean Langugage

   an informal introduction for English speakers

* Vocabulary

* Grammatical Items

The Korean Language

an informal introduction for English Speakers

by David Baxter[1]

General Remarks

The Korean language is spoken by 44 million people in South Korea, in addition to 22 million in North Korea and several million Koreans living in other countries, especially China (1.9 million), the United States (1.5 million), Japan (710,000), and the former Soviet Union (450,000)[2]. This makes it one of the twenty most commonly spoken languages in the world. Although scholars in China and Japan had for centuries taken a practical interest in Korean, Westerners first began to investigate the language in the late 19th century, as the previously tightly shut "hermit kingdom" of Korea began to open its harbors to Western countries, and missionaries from France, England and the United States came bringing Christianity. They wrote the first Korean grammars (Ross, 1877; Ridel, 1881; Underwood, 1890) and compiled the first Korean dictionaries (Ridel, 1881; Underwood, 1890). During the 20th century, significant contributions to the study of the Korean language have been made by Finnish G.J. Ramstedt and American Samuel Martin, among others.

Currently the Korean language is taught at approximately fifty American and Canadian universities, with more being added each year. It is also taught at more than 20 universities each in Europe and East Asia. As Korea's relationship with the West grows closer, and Korea plays an ever more important role in world economics and politics, it becomes more and more important for Westerners to understand the Korean people, along with their culture, history, and national identity. Understanding of the language, and how it differs from English, the *lingua franca* of the West, provides a vital key to this overall understanding[3].

The Korean language has undergone unprecedented turmoil during the 20th century. From 1910 to 1945, Korea was under Japanese Imperialist control, and the Japanese government waged a campaign to eliminate the Korean language and replace it with Japanese. All school classes were conducted in Japanese, and students were punished for even speaking Korean among themselves. Koreans were required to adopt Japanese names in order to have any rights as citizens. Due to the undying efforts of Korean linguists, novelists, poets, and other intellectuals, the Korean language was not obliterated, but it did adopt many Japanese words and phrases. Most of these have disappeared from use in the years since liberation in 1945, and some have been deliberately removed from the language and replaced with pure Korean expressions. Most of those that have remained are part of a spe-

---

[1] The author would like to express his deep appreciation to Professor Sang-Oak Lee of Seoul National University for his helpful insights and suggestions.

[2] The population figures listed here are official statistics from the end of 1992. There is some dispute over the number of ethnic Koreans in these countries, and the actual figures may be significantly higher. It should also be noted that not all ethnic Koreans living in other countries are fluent in Korean.

[3] In this paper, various aspects of the Korean language are explained through comparisons with English, as English is the native language of the author. It is hoped that this method of explanation will also be of help to readers for whom English is a second language.

cialized jargon of particular fields, and are not used by the population at large.

The division of the Korean peninsula into North and South following the end of World War II has caused the languages of the two Koreas to become substanstially different from each other. Whereas in the South the adoption of foreign vocabulary items and the use of Sino-Korean words has gone virtually unrestricted, the North has made a conscious effort to "purify" the language, by establishing a standard called the "Cultured Language," which substitutes words of native Korean origin with Sino-Korean and other loanwords. Whereas the South has chosen the dialect of the Seoul area for its standard, the North has chosen to model its official language after the dialect of the area including P'yŏngyang. As the citizens of the two Koreas have almost no contact with each other (The Korean War has never officially ended; the two sides are merely at an extended truce.), they occasionally have difficulty understanding one another when they do meet.

The standard language of the South is defined as the modern language of educated Seoulites. Due to the extreme population displacement during the Korean War, when millions of Koreans had to flee their homes, only about 20% of current Seoul residents can claim it as their family home of more than 50 years. The rest of the population is a mixture of people from all over the peninsula, many of whom retain a pronounced "accent" from their place of origin, just as someone from the American South might not lose his drawl if he moves to New England. Regional differences are most prominent in pronunciation and intonation, as the written language is the same throughout South Korea. Television is proving a great equalizer and homogenizer of Korean, as announcers and actors are all given thorough training in and expected to maintain a high level of faithfulness to the standard language. While this makes it more difficult to study the various Korean dialects, it does improve communication, especially for the non-native speaker.

Geneology/ Language Family

Geneologically, Korean is not even remotely related to English and the other Indo-European languages. It is most likely a distant cousin of the Altaic languages and Japanese, but if so, it diverged from them thousands of years ago, and the body of related vocabulary, while significant, is not very large. It appears that early forms of the Tungus, Mongolian, and Turkish language groups (members of the Altaic language family) share a common parent language, but Proto-Korean either diverged from it much earlier than the other three groups, or perhaps had a sibling relationship with it, both having diverged from an earlier common parent language. Japanese shares many grammatical characteristics with Korean, but the correspondence of sounds and the similarity of vocabulary and grammatical endings are too poor and infrequent to establish a definite genetic relationship between the two languages. The result of this linguistic isolation is that Korean has few cognate vocabulary items in common with other languages, with the exception of those that are the result of linguistic borrowing.

The only words likely to be familiar to English speakers are those that Korean has borrowed from English (and other Western languages) during the past century. These words were generally adopted along with the things or ideas they represent from Western culture.

When the Koreans brought something new from the West for which they did not have a name, they generally either adopted the original name (television, ice cream), or gave it a Sino-Korean name, taking advantage of the unusual productivity of the Chinese characters (a 'watch' is a 時計, or "time-measurer").

Writing System

alphabet

Korean is generally written in *han'gŭl* alphabet, which was invented by Sejong the Great (r. 1418-1450), the fourth king of the Chosŏn Period, in the early 15th century, according to phonetic and metaphysical principles, and based on careful linguistic observation and analysis of the Korean language. *han'gŭl* shows not only individual phonemes, but also how they are arranged into syllables. As a scientific invention, *han'gŭl* is unique among the world's writing systems, and Koreans are justifiably proud of it and its inventor.

For the consonant characters, Sejong classified the various sounds (phonemes) of Korean into categories based on how they are pronounced (manner of articulation) and where they are pronounced (place of articulation), much as is done in modern phonology. He modelled the basic character for each place of articulation on a visual image of how the speech organs look when in that particular position (See Figure 1). Thus the character for [k] (ㄱ) is a representation of the back of the tongue pulled up to touch the rear part of the roof of the mouth (the soft palate) of a left-facing speaker– exactly how one makes a [k] sound. The character for [n] (ㄴ) shows the tip of the tongue against the roof of the mouth behind the teeth (against the alveolar ridge), and the characters for sounds made in the throat are all based on a abstract representation of the throat (ㅇ). The fricative sounds (including [s], [z] and [ch]) were made with the tip of the tongue immediately behind the teeth, and were based on a character (ㅅ) modelled after the shape of a tooth. The basic character (ㅁ) for labials ("lip sounds" like [b], [m] and [p]) is most likely an adaptation of the Chinese character for 'mouth' (口). Given the derivation of the other basic consonant characters, however, it may very well be an abstract representation of the shape of the lips.

	Velar	Alveolar	Labial	Dental		Glottal
Plain	ㄱ [k]	ㄷ [t]	ㅂ [p]	ㅈ [ts]	ㅅ [s]	ㆆ [ʔ]
Heavily Aspirated	ㅋ [kʰ]	ㅌ [tʰ]	ㅍ [pʰ]	ㅊ [tsʰ]		ㅎ [h]
Unaspirated Tense	ㄲ [k']	ㄸ [t']	ㅃ [p']	ㅉ [ts']	ㅆ [s']	ㆅ [x]
Nasal	ㆁ [ŋ]	ㄴ [n]	ㅁ [m]			ㅇ

Figure 1. Some Original *Han'gŭl* Consonants

To show the different manners of articulation, Sejong devised a simple but ingeneous system. Let us take as an example the alveolar sounds (made with the tip of the tongue on the ridge behind the teeth). The basic character for this series is ㄴ ([n]), which is a nasal consonant. To make the character for the stop with the same place of articulation ([t]), a stroke is added to the top of the character: ㄷ. The heavily aspirated version of ㄷ ([tʰ]) has yet another stroke added: ㅌ. The unaspirated, tense version is made by writing the plain stop character twice: ㄸ. Thus stroke addition indicates a somehow stronger sound (either [+obstruent] or [+aspirated]), and reduplication indicates the feature [+tense].

For vowels, showing graphically how the various sounds are produced is much more difficult than with consonants, as in a vowel there is by definition no place in the mouth where the air flow is obstructed. To create characters for the vowels, Sejong turned to abstract concepts from East Asian philosophy, including Yin/Yang and the triad of Heaven, Earth, and Man. Here, too, he first created simple symbols for a few basic sounds, and constructed the other characters by combining them. Figure 2 is a chart of the three basic characters, with their pronunciation, tongue position, acoustic description, and symbolic source, as originally described by Sejong. Figure 3 shows how the basic characters are combined to represent other vowel sounds, including diphthongs and triphthongs. The Yin and Yang designations refer to orientation in terms of vowel harmony. When dots are placed above a horizontal line or to the right of a vertical line, the resulting vowel is Yang; when they are placed below or to the left of a line, the result is a Yin vowel.

Graph	Pronun-ciation	Tongue (position)	Voice	Symbolic Source
●	ʌ	contracted	deep	(round) heaven
—	ɨ	slightly contracted	not deep, not shallow	(flat) earth
|	i	not contracted	shallow	(upright) man

Figure 2. Basic Vowel Characters

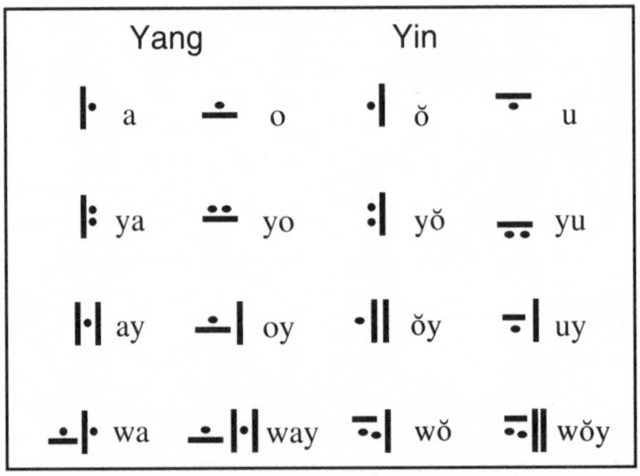

Figure 3. Combination Vowel Characters

The consonant and vowel characters are combined to form syllable units. The initial consonant (or ㅇ in syllables that begin with a vowel) is written first, followed by the vowel and a final consonant or consonants where necessary. Vowels whose main stroke is vertical are written to the right of the initial consonant, and those whose main stroke is horizontal are written beneath it. The following examples are written in modern script, in which the original dots have been replaced with easier-to-write short lines. Also, some diphthongs have become monophthongs, and they are transcribed here according to modern practice.

가 *ka*   간 *kan*   소 *so*   옥 *ok*

관 *kwan*   괜 *kwaen*   쇄 *swae*   꽤 *k'wae*

Although *han'gŭl* was created in the 15th century, it was not immediately adopted into widespread use. Classical Chinese was the preferred medium of written expression for the educated elite, and the new script was considered "undignified" in comparison. In addition, in threatened the monopoly that the upper classes held over the written word and made it possible for even women and peasants to become literate. In the beginning, *han'gŭl* was used mainly for writing novels and poetry in the vernacular and for annotations and transla-ition of texts written in classical Chinese. The everyday use of the alphabet spread very gradually from the women of the court to the upper class women, and finally to the lower classes as well. Most scholars continued to favor classical Chinese through the 19th century, and it was only at the beginning of this century that *han'gŭl* became dominant in every aspect of Koreans' writing.

non-han'gŭl *scripts*

In addition to *han'gŭl*, Koreans sometimes use the Roman alphabet to represent foreign words and abbreviations, Arabic numerals for numbers and calculations, and Chinese char-acters for Sino-Korean words and names.

If a foreign word has been adopted into the Korean language and is used commonly in everyday speech, it is generally written in *han'gŭl*. Foreign words not in general usage are used for a touch of real or perceived sophistication in brand names, etc., or to refer to a thing or idea still unfamiliar in Korea, and for which there is no commonly used name. In this case the word is often written first in *han'gŭl*, with the Roman alphabet spelling in parentheses following. The Roman alphabet is the standard for all foreign words, including those from languages such as Russian or Arabic, which are ordinarily written in other scripts.

Although classical Chinese has long since been replaced in actual use by written Korean, it is still taught in Korean middle and high schools. The Chinese characters are still used in newspaper headlines because of their conciseness and immediate semantic communicative power. They are also used sometimes for writing names (which are tradi-tionally Sino-Korean) and in scholarly writing because they do not have the ambiguity of a phonetic script like *han'gŭl*. There are many Chinese characters that have the same pronun-ciation in Korean, so if a Sino-Korean word or especially a Sino-Korean name is written in *han'gŭl*, it is not always clear which character is intended. There is a trend nowadays to avoid using Chinese characters whenever practical, and some newborns (especially girls) are even given pure Korean names.

Chinese characters were formerly used to represent numbers as well, but they have been almost entirely replaced by Arabic numerals. One can imagine three reasons for this change. First, Chinese characters are awkward for expressing quantities of more than one digit (one-hundred-two-ten-three vs. 123, etc.). Second, Arabic numerals stand out clearly to the eye and are immediately recognized as representing numbers, whereas the Chinese characters for numbers are not fundamentally different from other characters. Third, increasing contact with other countries has brought a need to adopt a number system recognized world-wide, not only in East Asia.

vertical vs. horizontal writing

When characters in any writing system are used to write texts, they are generally written either in horizontal rows or vertical columns. The characters in a row, or the columns on a page, may either be arranged from left to right, or from right to left. The vertical orientation in all writing systems is from top to bottom, rather than from bottom to top. Considering all the combinations of the two factors of rows vs. columns, and left vs. right horizontal orientation, there are thus four theoretically possible arangements for characters on a page. These are shown in Figure 4, in which rows and columns are outlined with boxes, and the order of the characters is shown with numerals.

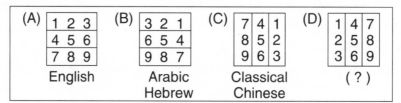

Figure 4. Horizontal and Vertical Writing Styles

(A) is of course the way in which English in written. Well known examples of (B) are Arabic and Hebrew. Classical Chinese is written as in (C), but the author knows of no language that uses (D).

Korean writing, both that using Chinese characters and that using *han'gŭl*, was originally written as in (C), following the model of classical Chinese. When only a few characters were to be written, as in the title of a document or on a stone marker, they were sometimes written in a horizontal row, also from right to left, as in (B). Beginning in the late 19th century, however, exposure to Western languages and a growing emphasis on speed and efficiency in reading led to attempts to write the Korean language as in (A). Due to the visual structure of Chinese characters and *han'gŭl*, which combine both horizontal and vertical elements in a roughly square shape, both scripts have proved easily adaptable to horizontal writing. The change from (C) to (A) has been gradual, but nowadays newspapers are virtually the only major publications to still use (C).[4]

---

[4] Many newspapers have begun to combine horizontal and vertical writing, and a few dailies (e.g. *Han-Kyoreh Shinmun*) use horizontal writing exclusively.

Phonology

vowels

Korean has between 7 and 10 monophthongs ("pure" vowels, in which the position of the mouth does not change during utterance), depending on the speaker. Standard Korean officially has 10 such vowels, although two of these (ü and ö) may also be pronounced as diphthongs (wi and we). In addition, many Koreans do not distinguish between the two vowels [e] and [ɛ]. The two Korean "o" sounds ([ŏ] and [ŏ]), which are clearly distinguished by all Koreans, are particularly hard for Americans to tell apart. American English, on the other hand, has relatively few pure vowels. American vowels usually involve a change of lip position (and therefore of vowel quality) at the end.

Korean vowels are always pronounced the same, and with more or less the same stress, whereas English vowels change quality depending on whether or not they are stressed. A comparison of the English and Korean words for "banana" clarifies this difference. In the pronunciation of the English word, the first and last syllables are unstressed, and so their vowel becomes the "schwa" sound "uh." The International Phonetic Association symbol for the vowel of the second syllable, which is stressed, is [æ], the vowel in "bat" and "man." In the Korean word, the vowel in each syallble is pronounced with the same quality and the same stress, much like the English exclamation "Ah!" Thus, while the pronunciation of the English word could be written "buh-næ-nuh," the pronunciation of the Korean word would more accurately be written "bah-nah-nah."

Vowel Harmony. Like the other Altaic languages, Korean has a system of "vowel harmony." The vowels are divided into two groups– the Yin vowels and the Yang vowels– and as a rule the two are not mixed in a single word. A few often used endings have two alternate forms: one for Yin stems and one for Yang. Perhaps the area in which vowel harmony plays the most important role is in onomatopoeic words– words that imitate or suggest what they stand for (e.g. "bang," "crunch," "slap"). These words often come in Yin/Yang pairs, of which the Yin variant refers to a larger action than the Yang variant. For example, a stone falling in a pond goes *p'ongdang* (Yang) whereas a rotund man plopping in the same lake would go *p'ungdŏng*(Yin)

consonants

The Korean [r] is a stranger to the American tongue (as is the American [r] to the Korean tongue). It is similar to the flapped [r] of Spanish, Italian, or Japanese. It cannot come at the end of a word, whereas the Korean [l] sound (slightly different from an American [l]) cannot come at the beginning. This kind of difference between English and Korean liquids (r's and l's) accounts for the difficulty that Koreans have with words like "light" and "right" when they learn English.

Korean has three different manners of articulation for its three word-initial unaspirated stops and one affricate (see Figure 1) at each place of articulation. In other words, there are three different p's, three different t's, three different k's, and three different ch's with which a word may start. Let us take [t] as an example. The plain version [t] is pronounced with a slight puff of breath (aspiration). There is also a heavily aspirated version [tʰ] and an unaspirated, tense version [t'] as well. The unaspirated, tense [t'] is very similar to [t] in French and Italian, and is close to the pronunciation of "t d" in English "Just do it."[5] It is somewhat harder for the English speaker to differentiate between the two aspirated stops [t] and [tʰ], as the amount of aspiration is not always the same, but rather varies from speaker to speaker and even with the same speaker according to his or her mood.

Korean distinguishes between two different "s" sounds, one "breathy" and one "tense." This is a very subtle difference that completely eludes most non-Koreans and even some Koreans (esp. those from the south-east).

Final Consonants. Word-final consonants in Korean are never released, whereas in English they sometimes are and sometimes aren't, with no difference in meaning. "Unreleasing" (as defined by Kim-Renaud 1974) means retaining the *oral* contact after articulation of a consonant. In Korean a consonant is released only when it is followed by a vowel within the same syllable. After saying a Korean word ending with [p] the lips should always be pressed together.

The fact that final consonants are not released has brought the side effect that all stops, fricatives, and affricates with the same place of articulation sound exactly the same when they come at the end of a syllable. This has created a large number of homonyms. One often-cited example is the seven different native Korean (not Sino-Korean) words all pronounced [nat]: 낟 'grain', 낱 'a unit', 낫 'sickle', 났- 'was born', 낮 'daytime', 낯 'face', and 낳- 'to give birth'.

Consonant Clusters. Like the other Altaic languages, Korean has limits in the number of consonants that can occur successively. Only one consonant can be pronounced at the beginning of a syllable, and only one at the end, for a maximum total of two consonants in a row (the final consonant of one syllable plus the initial consonant of the next syllable). When English words with more than one initial consonants are pronounced in Korean, a vowel [ɨ] is inserted between the consonants: strike > *sitiraiki*.

rhythm, stress, and pitch

English has a very intricate system of word-stress and sentence-stress, and the amount of time between sentence stresses is usually about the same regardless of how many syllables come between them. Which syllable is stressed often shows whether the word is being used as a verb or noun (e.g. reláy (verb), rélay (noun)).

In Korean, each syllable is pronounced with about the same amount of stress and takes about the same amount of time to pronounce. This does not mean that Korean is spoken in a monotonous drone, but rather that changes in rhythm, stress, and pitch do not usually result in a change of lexical or syntactic meaning. Changes of intonation *are* used at the ends of sentences to differentiate between statements and questions, much as they are in English.

---

[5] As pronounced in Nike™ advertisements.

Morphology

vocabulary/ word formation

The source of the Korean language's most basic, everyday vocabulary is the language to which present-day Korean traces its roots: the Shilla[6] language. The vast majority of its high-level vocabulary however, including almost all conceptual and academic terms, consists of Sino-Korean words— words consisting of combinations of Chinese characters. As written Chinese was associated with the educated elite, words of Chinese origin are often more polite and formal than their native Korean synonyms. They also are more stiff and impersonal. In addition to words employing the Chinese characters, there has been a small but significant amount of linguistic borrowing from spoken Chinese, Mongolian, Japanese, and most recently, English. The borrowings have occurred primarily during periods of military occupation or strong cultural influence by other civilizations.

Chinese characters were probably first introduced to the Korean peninsula around 2000 years ago, and were originally used to write only the Chinese language. Each Chinese character is a pictograph, a symbol representing a particular word with a particular pronunciation and meaning. This means that there is a different character for each basic word, for a total of over 50,000. Only about two or three thousand characters are used commonly in Korea, however, and knowledge of 10,000 characters is considered exceptional.

Chinese characters have been used in Japan[7] and Vietnam, in addition to Korea and China itself, and each country adapted the pronunciation of the characters to its own phonetic system while retaining the meanings more or less intact. The characters can be combined almost limitlessly in strings of two or three to produce very short words with very specific meanings. The vast majority of Sino-Korean words consist of two Chinese characters. Some of these words were adopted whole from China (mainly in pre-modern times) or Japan (mainly in the 20th century), resulting in identical vocabulary in the three languages, with slightly different pronunciation. Other words were created in Korea from previously introduced characters, with the result that in Korea an 'engagement' is usually referred to as a 'Promise to Marry (約婚),' while in Japan it is a 'Marriage Promise (婚約).' The Chinese words for 'steam ship' and 'train' are 'Fire Wheel Ship (火輪船)' and 'Fire Wheel Car (火輪車)', while in Korean and Japan they are 'Steam Ship (汽船)' and 'Steam Car (汽車).' Still other "Chinese" characters have been created in Korea. The character 乭 (meaning 'rock,' pronounced *tol* consists of the Chinese character for 'rock' (石) on top of another character (乙) used to show the final *l* of the Korean word. The character 畓, meaning 'rice paddy,' is a similar combination of the Chinese character for 'water' (水) and the character for 'field' (田), as a rice paddy is basically a field flooded with water.

word endings

All derivation and verb conjugation in Korean is accomplished through the addition of

---

6 One of the "Three Kingdoms" on the Korean Peninsula in the first centuries A.D., Shilla conquered Koguryŏ and Paekje in the 7th century, uniting the peninsula for the first time.

7 Chinese characters were first brought to Japan around 400 A.D. by the Korean scholar Wani, pronounced Wangin in Korean.

various endings to a stem or root. For predicates (i.e. verbs and adjectives), the basic meaning is always contained in the root, while the endings show grammatical function, part of speech, tense, aspect, honorific level, etc. All Korean sentences end in a predicate, and the fact that so much information is included as part of the predicate makes it possible for a sentence in Korean to consist of a single verb or adjective, and its endings.

1) Haengbokha-shi-gess-ŏyo. 'You must be happy.'

2) Chap-hi-dŏ-nya? 'Did it get caught?'

In these word-sentences, the first part (the root) gives the respective basic meanings of 1) 'happy' and 2) 'to catch,' while the last part is part of an honorific system showing how careful and polite the speaker is being toward the hearer. In 1), the speaker is being quite polite(-ŏyo), while the speaker in 2) is most likely an older person addressing a child(-nya). In 1), -shi- indicates that the speaker considers the implied subject (here, the person addressed) worthy of respect, while -gess- shows that the statement made is a matter of conjecture, rather than established fact. In 2), -hi- makes the active verb 'to catch' become passive('to be caught'), and-dŏ-indicates past tense of first-hand experience. These two examples are relatively simple, with only three endings apiece, but there is theoretically no limit to the number of possible combinations of endings, and strings of five or more are not uncommon.

Due to this highly developed system of endings, Korean uses pronouns much less than English and other Western languages do, and in fact has no relative pronouns at all. Predicate endings give so much information about subjects and objects that the hearer usually knows what or whom the speaker is referring to without explicit reference. Development in the written language of a female third person pronoun corresponding to "she"(kŭnyŏ)has taken place in the 20th century, due largely to exposure to Western languages and translations of Western novels, but this pronoun is rarely used in the spoken language, as there is simply no need for it.

Luckily for the student of Korean, the Korean language does not have gender categories for nouns, and it also has no articles (the equivalents of "a", "an", and "the"). These two facts alone mean that the student of Korean need not worry about many of the difficulties one faces when learning a European language.

Syntax

word order

The basic word order for English is S-V-O; the subject is followed by the verb, which is followed by the direct object: "I eat the apple." The basic order of a Korean sentence is S-O-V: "I the apple eat." In fact, except for the subject coming towards the beginning of the sentence, almost everything about Korean word order is backwards from an English speaker's point of view. Modifying words and phrases come before the word they modify, instead of after them, as in English. English has prepositions, Korean has suffixes which function as "post-positions."

The following sentence, taken from a recent Korean newspaper, serves to illustrate just how different Korean word order is from that of English. Here is the whole sentence, followed by a romanized version and a fairly literal English translation:

유엔안전보장이사회는 北韓核문제를 놓고 中國측이 결의안 대신 安保理의장 성명으로 대신할 것을 요구해 상임이사국들간에 막후절충을 벌이고 있으나 美國 은 결의안채택을 강행할 방침인 것으로 5일 알려졌다.[8]

Yuen-anjŏn-bojang-isa-hoe-nŭn Puk-han-haek-munje-rŭl no-k'o Chung-gŭk-ch'ŭk-i kyŏrŭl-an taeshin Anbori-ŭijang sŏngmyŏng-ŭro taeshinhal kŏs-ŭl yogu-hae sang-in-isa-guk-dŭl-gan-e makhu-jŏlch'ung-ŭl pŏri-go iss-ŭna Miguk-ŭn kyŏrŭi-an-ch'aet'aek-ŭl kang-haeng-hal pangch im-in kŏs-ŭro o-il allyŏjŏtta.

It became known on the 5th that the U.N. Security Council is holding behind-the-scenes negotiations among (its) permanent member nations concerning the problem of North Korean nuclear (capability), as China has requested that the resolution (currently under consideration) be replaced with a statement from the head of the Security Council, but the United States is planning to force the adoption of the resolution.

This is a very long and complex sentence, but sentences of this type are the norm rather than the exception in academic or journalistic writing, and are not difficult for the educated Korean to understand.

Analysis of this sentence shows that it consists of three large parts. I have shown them in the order in which they appear in the Korean sentence (hereafter in romanization only), followed by the English translation with a number in parentheses representing that section's position in the English sentence.

1. Yuen-anjŏn-bojang-isa-hoe-hŭn Puk-haek-munje-rŭl no-k'o Chung-guk-ch'ŭk-i kyŏrŭi-an taeshin Anbori-ŭijang sŏnginyŏng-ŭro taeshinhal kŏs-ŭl yogu-hae sang-im-isa-guk-dŭl-gan-e makhu-jŏlch'ung-ŭl pŏri-go iss-ŭna
the U.N. Security Council is holding behind-the-scenes negotiations among (its) permanent member nations concerning the problem of North Korean nuclear (capability), as China has requested that a resolution be replaced with a statement from the head of the Security Council, but (2)

2. Miguk-ŭn kyŏrŭi-an-ch'aet'ask-ŭl kanghaeng-hal pangch'im-i-
the United States is planning to force the adoption of a resolution.(3)

3. -n kŏs-ŭro o-il allyŏjŏtta.
It became known on the 5th that(1)

The last section of the Korean sentence must be translated first to render a smooth English equivalent. "It became known that.." is a passive verb construction without a real

8 中央日報 (*The Joong-ang Daily News*), Thursday, May 6, 1993, p. 2.

subject. The main predicate of a Korean sentence always comes at the very end, whereas in English it almost always comes near the beginning, immediately after the subject.

The first two large sections of the Korean text appear in the same order in the English equivalent, but the conjunction "but" (na) is attached to the last word of the first section in Korean, while in English it should begin the next clause. The same is true of "that" (-n kŏs-ŭro)in section 3.

Further analysis of the rather complex first section reveals greater difference in the structure of Korean and English:

1. *Yuen-anjŏn-bojang-isa-hoe-nŭn*
   the U.N. Security Council(1)

2. *Puk-han-haek-munje-rŭl no-k'o*
   concerning the problem of North Korean nuclear(capability),(4)

3. *Chung-guk-ch'ŭk-i*
   [as] China(5)

4. *kyŏrŭi-an taeshin*
   [instead of]a resolution(7)

5. *Anbori-ŭijang sŏngmyŏng-ŭro taeshinha-*
   be replaced with a statement from the head of the Security Council,(8)

6. *-l kŏs-ŭl yogu-hae*
   has reuested that(6)

7. *sang-im-isa-guk-dŭl-gan-e*
   among(its)permanent member nations(3)

8. *makhu-jŏlch'ung-ŭl pŏri-go iss-ŭna*
   is holding behind-the-scenes negotiations[but](2)

The main thing to notice here is that once again the predicates come at the end in Korean, and imediately after the subject in English. The reader of the Korean sentence knows immediately that the U.N. Security Council is the subject of this clause, but does not know *what* the Security Council is doing until the end of the section. On the other hand, the reader of the English version knows that the Security Council is holding negotiations, but does not find out exactly *why* until the end of the section. In general, the structure of an English sentence begins with the broadest concepts and fills in the details later, while a Korean sentence gives the reader a lot of details at the beginning and then places them in context. Since the constructions that make a sentence negative are attached to the predicate, the reader of a Korean sentence occasionally makes his way all the way through a long sentence only to find that the sentence means exactly the opposite of what he had thought.

For further reference, I have divided the same sentence into 28 small parts, none of which come in the same order in English as in Korean. In several cases I have even had to separate a verb stem from an ending in Korean. One lesson the English-speaking student of Korean can learn from this example is that it is virtually impossible to read a Korean sentence of this complexity while simultaneously translating everything into English. In order to attain any degree of fluency in Korean, it is necessary to "think in Korean," processing Korean data without needing to translate into one's native language. This is equally true for the Korean student of English.

1. *Yuen-anjŏn-bojang-isa-hoe-hŭn*	4. the U.N. Security Council
2. *Puk-han-haek*	12. of <u>North Korean nuclear</u> (capability),
3. *munje*	11. the problem
4. *-rŭl no-k'o*	10. concerning
5. *Chung-guk-ch'ŭk-i*	13. (as) <u>China</u>
6. *kyŏrŭi-an taeshin*	16. [instead of] a resolution
7. *Anbori*	22. of the <u>Security Council</u>,
8. *ŭijang*	21. from the head
9. *sŏngmyŏng*	20. a statement
10. *-ŭro*	19. with
11. *taeshinha-*	18. replaced
12. *-l*□	17. be
13. *kŏs-ŭl*	15. that
14. *yogu-hae*	14. has requested
15. *sang-im-isa-guk-dŭl*	9. (its) permanent member nations
16. *gan-e*	8. among
17. *makhu-jŏlch'ung-ŭl*	7. behind-the-scenes negotiations
18. *pŏri-go*	6. holding
19. *iss-*	5. is
20. *-ŭna Miguk-ŭn*	23. but the <u>United States</u>
21. *kyŏrŭi-an*	28. of a resolution.
22. *ch'aet'aek-ŭl*	27. the adoption
23. *kanghaeng-ha-*	26. force
24. *-l*	25. to
25. *pangch'im-i-*	24. is planning
26. *-n kŏs-ŭro*	3. that
27. *o-il*	2. on the 5th
28. *allyŏjŏtta.*	1. It became known

This sentence also serves as a good example of how Chinese characters are used in journalistic writing. Of the twenty-eight parts shown above, nineteen are composed mainly or entirely of Sino-Korean elements, and thus could be written either in Chinese characters or in *han'gŭl*. Only four are written in Chinese characters (2, 5, 7, and 20– words originally written in Chinese characters and their English translations underlined above), and these are ones that contain the proper nouns "North Korea" (北韓), "China" (中國), "Security Council" (安保理), and "United States" (美國). "Nuclear" (核) is also written with a Chinese character, as it is a Sino-Korean word and is attached to the word for "North Korea" to make a compound. The Chinese characters for "Security Council" in no. 7 are actually an abbreviation of the complete title, found in no. 1. The abbreviation is written in Chinese characters for clarity, whereas when the same word is spelled out in no. 1, han'gŭl suffices.

Semantics

speech levels & social background

America and Korea have two extremely different social histories. The United States was founded on the idea that all people are created equal, and as a nation has been dedicated at least in principle to equality ever since. This idea is reflected in the fact that Americans can use the same sentence when speaking to the president, to parents and grandparents, to friends, to children, or to a stranger.

In Korea, this is impossible. Confucianism was adopted hundreds of years ago, and has implanted in Korean society the idea that everyone and everything has a particular place. Not always is the person you are talking to on the same social level as you. Whether because of age, profession, social status or whatever, he or she is often either "higher" or "lower" than you, and should be spoken to accordingly.

The Korean language reflects this social phenomenon in its system of "levels of speech" Before significant contact with the West began at the end of the 19th century, there were as many as six distinct levels in the language, each to be used by certain types of people to certain types of people. The 20th century has brought the spread of democracy and the gradual demise of Confucianism, and today's young people commonly use only two or three different levels of speech in their everyday lives, but the heirarchy remains in the language in many forms. The basic word for "you" is nŏ, but it can be used only when addressing a child or a close acquaintance the same age or younger than oneself. For other people, one must choose from an assortment of titles including "teacher", "aunt/uncle", "older brother/sister", and several more polite words that just mean "you."

head vs. heart

Many people familiar with both English and Korean would agree that if English is language of the head, Korean is a language of the heart. English tends to have clear and clean distinctions between definitions, whereas Korean is much more subtle and subjective. A telling example of this trend may be found in the words describing different colors. On an objective level, there are relatively few purely Korean color adjectives.[9] In addition to black and white, the spectrum is divided up into the three primary colors of red, yellow, and blue. The same word p'uruda, can be used equally effectively to describe both green grass and a blue sky.

The subjective level, however, is where Korean color words shine. Using consonants of different strengths, vowels of different colors, and various suffixes added to the adjective stem, the Koreans can express how a certain color makes them *feel*. The extent and subtle-

---

[9] The native Korean color adjectives are supplemented extensively by Sino-Korean words and native compound nouns consisting of the name of something followed by the word for 'Color' 빛 (e.g. 쪽빛 'indigo-color').

ty to which this is possible goes far beyond the difference between English "blue" and "bluish," and is in fact one of the characteristics that makes the Korean language unique. Similar shades of distinction are made in words describing tastes. Koreans at first have a hard time believing that English speakers use the same word "hot" to describe both coffee and chili peppers.

ego

From a Korean perspective, the English speaker is decidedly ego-centric. He speaks of "my home," "my mother," "my school," and "my country," while a Korean sees these as belonging to a group of people (family, students, or citizens), and always precedes them with a possessive pronoun meaning 'our.'[10] Ask a Korean about his job, and he will usually tell you first what company he works for, then what section he is in and what his rank is. An English speaker, on the other hand, will most likely first tell you what he personally does ("I'm an electrician," etc.). To the Korean, membership in a particular section or company is of primary importance, while to the English speaker, his own skills or duties come first, and the company is seen as an entity for which he provides a service and from which he expects due compensation. The contrast between Eastern self-effacement and Western self-assertion is also evident in the way Koreans and English speakers express subjective judgements. In general, the English speaker makes himself the subject of the sentence, saying "I like chocolate," or "I hope it rains," while the Korean makes the object of judgement the subject of the sentence, saying "(As for me) chocolate is good," and "It would be nice if it rained."

---

[10] An extreme example of this is the fact that a Korean man will often refer to his wife as "our wife." This is, however, most likely a restricted form of our" actually including only the speaker himself, and does not imply wife-sharing.

References

Kang, Shin-Hang(1974, translation and annotation) Hunmin *Chŏngeum*(Correct Sounds for the Instruction of the People), Shin-gu Mun-go, Seoul

Kang, Shin-Hang(1990)*Kugŏhak-sa*(A History of Korean Linguistics), Posŏng Munhwa-sa, Seoul.

Ledyard, Gari K. (1966) The Korean Language Reform of 1446: *The Origin, Background, and Early History of the Korean Alphabet*, Ph.D. dissertation, University of California, Berkeley.

Lee, Ik-Sŏp(1986) *Kugŏ-hak Kaesŏl*(An Introduction to Korean Linguistics), Hakyŏn-sa Seoul.

Lee, Ki-Moon(1972) *Kugŏ-sa Kaesŏl*, Kaejŏng-p'an)(An Introduction to the History of the Korean Language, Revised Edition), Pagoda Publishers, Seoul.

Lee, Ki-Moon(1988) *Han'gŭl Match'um-pŏp mit Py'ojun-ŏ Kyujŏng Haesŏl*(Annotated *Han'gŭl* Orthoraphy and Standard Language Paradigms), Korean Language Research Center, Seoul.

Lee, Ki-Moon(1991) *Kugŏ Ŏhwi-sa Yŏn-gu* (Studies in Korean Lexical History, Tong-a Publishers, Seoul.

Lee, Sang-Oak (1982) "The Theory of Altaic Languages and Korean," *Korea Journal* 22.1: 14-19

Lee, Sang-Oak (1993) *Graphical Ingenuity in the Korean Writing System: with New Reference to Calligraphy.* Presented at the Symposium on the Korean Writing System, George Washington University, Washington, D.C, August 6-8, 1992.

Martin, S.E. (1951) 'Korean Phonemics,' in *Language* 27.4.

Nam, Ki-Shim & Ko, Young-Gŏn(1987) *Py'ojun Kugŏ Munpŏp-ron* (Standard Korean Grammar), Pagoda Publishers, Seoul.

Ramstedt, G.J. (1928) 'Remarks on the Korean Language,' in *Mémoires de la Société Finno-Ougrienne* 58.

Ramstedt, G.J. (1939) *A Korean Grammar*, Helsinki.

Ramstedt, G.J. (1949) 'Studies in Korean Etymology,' in *Mémoires de la Société Finno-Ougrienne* 95.

Ridel, Félix Clair (1880) *Dictionnaire Coréen-Français*, Yokohama.

Ridel, Félix Clair (1881) *Grammaire Coréenne*, Yokohama.

Ross, John (1877) *Corean Primer*, Shanghai.

Sampson, Geoffrey (1985) *Writing Systems*, Stanford University Press, Stanford.

Underwood, H.G. (1890) *A Concise Dictionary of the Korean Language*, Yokohama.

Underwood, H.G. (1890) *An Introduction to the Korean Spoken Language*, Yokohama.

Vocabulary

(Numbers refer to pages.)

ㄱ

ㄴ

ㄷ

ㅈ

ㅊ

Grammatical Items
(Numbers refer to pages.)

Grammatical Items

(Roman numbers(I, II, III) refers to books
and Arabic numbers(1, 2, 3···)to lessons.)

집필	총괄	이상억	서울대 인문대 국문과 및 어학연구소
	1권	한미선	서울대 대학원 및 뉴욕주립대
	2권	윤희원	서울대 사범대 국어교육과
	3권	한재영	울산대 국문과 및 서울대 어학연구소
	보조	최은규	서울대 어학연구소
삽화/사진		이은미	
영어교열		David Baxter	서울대 인문대 국문과

Korean through English 1 한국어 1

발행일 / 1992년 11월 24일 제1판 1쇄
1997년 4월 10일 제2판 2쇄

편찬 / **서울대학교 어학연구소**
서울특별시 관악구 신림동 산 56-1
전화 : 880-5483

저작권자 / **대한민국 문화체육부**
서울특별시 종로구 세종로 82-1
전화 : 720-4926, 722-1328

발행 / **(주) 한림출판사**
서울특별시 종로구 관철동 13-13
Tel : 735-7554 Fax : 730-5149

미국 동시 발행 / **HOLLYM International Corp.**
18 Donald Place, Elizabeth, NJ 07208
Tel : (908)353-1655 Fax : (908)353-0255